CULTIVATING *Holy Beauty*

BOOK 2: *Letting the Healer Heal*

This Book Belongs to:

....

By Jessie North
www.CultivatingHolyBeauty.com

Cultivating Holy Beauty: Letting the Healer Heal

Copyright © 2018 Jessie North

All rights reserved. No portion of this book may be translated into other languages, reproduced in any form or by any electronic or mechanical means, including information storage and retrieval systems, without permission in writing from the author, except by reviewers, who may quote brief passages in a review.

ISBN 978-1-7321196-2-8

Scripture quotations marked NIV are taken from The Holy Bible, New International Version®, NIV®. Copyright © 1973, 1978, 1984, 2011 by Biblica, Inc.® Used by permission of Zondervan. All rights reserved worldwide. www.Zondervan.com

Scripture quotations marked ESV are taken from the ESV® (The Holy Bible, English Standard Version®). Copyright © 2001 by Crossway, a publishing ministry of Good News Publishers. Used by permission. All rights reserved.

Scripture quotations marked KJV are taken from the King James Version, Public domain.

Scripture quotations marked NKJV are taken from The Holy Bible, The New King James Version (NKJV®). Copyright © 1979, 1980, 1982, Thomas Nelson Publishers. Used by permission. All rights reserved.

Scripture quotations marked NASB are taken from the New American Standard Bible®. Copyright © 1960, 1962, 1963, 1968, 1971, 1972, 1973, 1975, 1977, 1995 by The Lockman Foundation. Used by permission. (www.Lockman.org)

Scripture quotations marked NLT are taken from The Holy Bible, New Living Translation. Copyright © 1996, 2004, 2007, 2013 by Tyndale House Foundation. Used by permission of Tyndale House Publishers, Inc., Carol Stream, Illinois 60188. All rights reserved.

Scripture quotations marked MSG [or The Message] are taken from The Message. Copyright © by Eugene H. Peterson 1993, 1994, 1995, 1996, 2000, 2001, 2002. Used by permission of Tyndale House Publishers, Inc., Carol Stream, Illinois 60188. All rights reserved.

Third Printing May 2021

Visit www.CultivatingHolyBeauty.com

Contents

Acknowledgements v

A Note from the Author vii

Are you the Group Leader? ix

    Group Basics x

    Course Record xi

    Guidelines for A Successful Group xii

    Addressing Hard Topics xiv

    I Want Jesus! xv

Lesson 1 Healing with Jesus 1

Lesson 2 Faith in the Healer 23

Lesson 3 The Purge 41

Lesson 4 Flip It 67

Lesson 5 Repentance and Forgiveness 85

Lesson 6 Forgiving Self 103

Lesson 7 Love Letters 121

Lesson 8 The Power of Choice 141

Lesson 9 Your Living Testimony 159

Appendix 179

Course Record 181

About the Author 182

Quiet Time Worksheet 184

My Battle Field Worksheet 186

Memory Verse Cards 188

Acknowledgements

Father,

Thank You for sending the most important person in my life to save me, Your Son, Jesus. You never withheld your love from me. You are always willing to meet me where I am, all the while lovingly walking me into a new understanding of Your heart. I can't wait to see what tomorrow holds! Jesus, I'm so thankful it's You.

Thank You, Father, for my husband, Adam—one of Your best soldiers. He loves and cares for me and our children with all he has. He is always willing to let me be me, even when it's hard. From childhood friend to life-long lover, thank You, Father, for choosing him. Adam, I'm so glad it's you!

Thank You for our children. I praise You for blessing them with patience, faithfulness, and courageous hearts for truth, purity, and adventure. I praise You Father for blessing my life with theirs. You could have given them to anyone, but You chose me to be their mother. They are more than I deserve! Noah and Bowen, I'm so glad it's you!

Father, I thank You for the countless volunteers who helped in getting this work ready to be published! Thank You for the women who allowed me to be a part of their journey, and for sharing their stories on the pages of Cultivating Holy Beauty. Please bless them all, Father!

I love You,

Jessie

Welcome to Letting the Healer Heal
A NOTE FROM THE AUTHOR

Dear Sister,

I am so excited for the journey ahead as you learn how to let the Healer reveal and heal the brokenness in your life. *Why does this matter so much?* Sometimes the source of our pain is obvious and palpable—never leaving us alone—like the throbbing of a smashed thumb. Other times, pain can lurk beyond the shadows, only to be noticed when someone accidentally bumps into it. The point is, no matter your background, we all have heart wounds to some degree. Jesus came to bind up the wounds of the heart so that we may walk in greater freedom(Isaiah 61:1-3)! Don't let the enemy tell you this doesn't apply to you!

Book 2, "Letting the Healer Heal", is designed to do just that! To point you to Jesus in such an undeniable way that you allow His Spirit to reveal wounds and lies that you have believed, no matter how big or small. This harbored hurt keeps you from knowing your worth and value to God.

What if you could be set free from the lies that keep you oppressed, suppressed, repressed and depressed? At one point or another, I have felt the effects of all of these in varying degrees—leaving me pouring into my family and others from an empty vessel and feeling like I was running out of air.

Do any of those apply to you? If so, then this book can help you step into the freedom Jesus died to give you! No matter the situation you find yourself in, Jesus is ALWAYS the answer. You just need to know how to find His gaze in the storm. "Letting the Healer Heal" will give you the tools needed to point you to Jesus in hard times, no matter how big or small, so you can walk in fellowship and freedom with Him.

To the degree you are willing to be vulnerable with Jesus is the degree He can heal you in this way. Don't hold back! He is worth it! You are worth it!

May I be found with my Jesus,

Jessie

Oppress—mental pressure or distress

Suppress—to prevent development

Repress—to restrain or inhibit

Depress—to push or pull down in a lower position through condemnation and accusation

Are you the Group Leader?

A FEW THINGS YOU NEED TO KNOW

Discussing these details up front will help you have a successful group. *Cultivating Holy Beauty* (CHB) consists of two parts:

- Part I of the *Cultivating Holy Beauty* series focuses on your vertical relationship with God and consists of three books:

    1. Book 1: Intimacy with Jesus
    2. Book 2: Letting the Healer Heal
    3. Book 3: Walking In the New or "W.I.N."

    This portion of the series can take an average of 35 weeks, not including breaks for vacations and holidays.

- Part II (coming in the future) focuses on your identity in Jesus and your horizontal relationships such as how you view yourself, marriage and motherhood.

- The skills taught in *Cultivating Holy Beauty* build upon one another. Be sure to complete the books in order for maximum benefit.

Group Basics

PREPARING FOR YOUR GROUP

- Welcome to "Letting the Healer Heal," the next step in your journey of growing closer to God!.

- By now your group may have gone down in number—please don't be discouraged. Trust that God used you in just the right way, at just the right time!

- The group meeting time should still be at least two hours. More time may be needed depending on the number of people in your group. Be intentional and respectful by beginning and ending on time.

- Save extra sharing and conversation for the end. This will ensure people with obligations to husbands, children, or otherwise will be able to leave on time. Discuss the time expectations at the beginning to allow clear expectations and accountability.

- Take time to discuss if adjustments need to be made for your meeting time. You are likely now in a new time of year and schedules may be changing.

- Remember to set a backup day for your group to meet if someone will need to miss the regular meeting time, along with a backup group leader if the current leader has to miss.

- Purposing to make the meeting as stress-free as possible is key in helping your group members complete the course successfully.

- If someone needs to miss a meeting, the group leader should meet with them one-on-one, either in person or over the phone, to help them catch up.

- Discuss with your group and decide who would be comfortable leading in your absence.

- While "Letting the Healer Heal" has nine lessons, you may decide to take more than one week on certain lessons, moving at the pace of the group. True transformation is a process and cannot be rushed. However, taking longer than two weeks on a lesson can cause the group to lose momentum. Be mindful not to sit too long in one spot.

- Follow the Leader's Guide at the beginning of each lesson. It has been field-tested and will help you stay on track and lead successful groups.

- A Participant's Guide is also provided to help the group members understand how to complete the lesson.

- Pray for your group members throughout the week, being sure to keep communication flowing through texting or phone calls.

- Just as true transformation is a process, leadership is also a process. Allow yourself to grow and be cultivated as a leader.

Course Record

BOOK 2

The "Course Record" form on page 181 may be a challenge for some. The below items are recommended before moving to the next book. The books build on one another. Please be sure to complete each book before moving to the next.

- Finish all nine lessons
- Memorize nine Scripture passages
- Record four or more Quiet Times a week

SPECIAL NOTE: Memorization may be a challenge for some. Having the verses memorized word perfect is not a prerequisite for finishing the course. Your best effort is enough!

Guidelines for A Successful Group

The following are recommended guidelines for a successful *Cultivating Holy Beauty* (CHB) group:

- Follow the Leader's Guide, being sure to prioritize:
    1. Worship
    2. Prayer
    3. Sharing Quiet Times

- Start on time. Beginning group time worshipping through music not only helps busy hearts and minds settle and focus on God, but it also helps ensure anyone running late won't miss the lesson discussion time.

- As worship comes to a close, the group leader should transition into prayer, modeling the WAR method of prayer for the group (Worship, Admit, Request). After Lesson 5, the group will begin participating in the WAR method of prayer together.

- After the prayer time has ended, give a quick summary of the lesson from your notes written on the Leader's Guide page.

- Share Quiet Times each week following the format on page 31 of Book 1, "Intimacy with Jesus." Always encourage every member to share, although some may not be comfortable in the beginning. Continue to find ways to support and encourage participation from all members.

- Following the Leader's Guide, in the second half of group time be sure to:
    1. Share answers to the questions picked by the leader.
    2. Share Hurt Letters and Love Letters as participants are willing (beginning in Lesson 3 and Lesson 7).
    3. Discuss the "Review" and "Before Your Next Lesson" sections.
    4. Recite memory verses.

- While we want to keep the group on track, sometimes God has plans of His own that we shouldn't overthrow. There may be times when the group ministers to one particular member who is in need of having truth spoken into them, and it takes the whole meeting. Don't be afraid to let this happen! God is growing leader's in these moments as they minster to the hurting people around them with their new skills. It's not hard to recognize when the Holy spirit is moving vs. someone just wanting to talk. Again, don't be afraid to let God take over.

- If someone is willing to share a Hurt Letter or Love Letter, allow this to take the place of answering the questions you highlighted. Often, healing takes place in the sharing of Hurt Letters and Love Letters and this should be considered a priority.

- If time allows, discuss your highlighted questions marked on the Leader's Guide. Encourage the participant's to share their answers. Often times, you will find yourself being the one who speaks the least in the group because of the sharing that is taking place. This is a good sign that the Holy Spirit is doing more leading than the group leader!

- Keep the group on track. Pay attention to when the group is getting off topic. The leader should gently direct the conversation back to the study. Additional conversation can take place once the purpose for the group time has been met.

- The leader should make sure the meeting ends at the set time, being respectful of group members, family, or child care workers who may be waiting for them. If you find more time is needed for the lesson, make sure the group agrees to stay longer or use the next week's meeting time to pick up where you left off.

- Give grace to those who are experiencing unusual circumstances and need more time to complete the lesson.

- The group should be a safe place to share Quiet Times and struggles without condemnation or judgment. What is shared in the group should be kept confidential. Always ask group members before any information is shared with a spouse, pastor, or anyone else.

Addressing Hard Topics

- Discipleship is often messy. Sometimes it means you feel like you are fighting harder for someone else's walk with God than they are. This "fight" however, is done in prayer—not in person.

- As a leader, remember that you don't have to have it all figured out! Don't be afraid to let your group member's minister to you when you are struggling. Be raw and real with them—it will only encourage them in their own struggles!

- Some group participants may choose not to share their Hurt Letters—this is okay! Don't pry and continue encouraging them to grow their trust in the Lord. The exercise of writing Hurt Letters and Love Letters is about growing trust between them and God. If you push for them to share, it may hinder their trust with you and the Lord.

- If you still have a non-believer in your group, praise the Lord they have stayed this long! Keep praying for them. Don't be afraid to check in with them every so often to see how they are, and if they are ready to receive Jesus into their hearts. Don't forget this is God's plan.

- Making disciples is one of the greatest privileges we have. But at times it can get messy, feel scary, and even seem risky. It's important to remember that God didn't give us a spirit of timidity—but of power and love (2 Timothy 1:7)! If you are feeling overwhelmed at leading a group or by a situation in your group, this may be a sign you are striving in your own strength. Take your eyes off of your group and put them back on Jesus! Your task as a *Cultivating Holy Beauty* Leader is to first, continue growing in your relationship with Jesus, and second, teach other's to do the same by living out your love for Jesus in front of others! As disciple-makers, this is all we can do!

- *Cultivating Holy Beauty* does not authorize anyone to give professional counseling advice. This course provides skills to deeply know and love your Savior—teaching others to do the same.

- No part of *Cultivating Holy Beauty* should be used to replace professional medical care. If you feel someone is showing signs of hurting themselves or is in any danger, don't wait or second guess yourself! Reach out to your pastor, women's ministry leader or someone that you know who can offer support right away!

I Want Jesus!

A SIMPLE PLAN OF SALVATION

- If you have someone in your group who is not yet a Christian and still has not made the decision to receive Jesus into their hearts, keep praying for them and pointing them to Jesus at every turn! This is a precious opportunity for you to gently walk them into a beautifully intimate relationship with the Lord. God is the one in control, so rest in His plan for this group member.

- Continue not to push for them to "pray the prayer" and instead rejoice that they are still hanging in there! There is a reason why they haven't made the leap yet, which will likely be uncovered soon if they allow God to show them. Don't underestimate the ways of the God of all Creation. His ways are higher—just believe He has a plan!

- Pray for them. Pray that they show up each week, and that they are doing the work. If they keep coming back, trust that God is softening their heart!

- Don't be afraid to check in with them every so often to see how they are doing and if they have any questions about salvation. The biggest way to have an impact on an unbeliever is by living out your love for Jesus in front of them! Movements of God fly on the wings of testimonies! Be sensitive to the Spirit and honest with your own struggles all while letting them see that your hope comes from Jesus!

- If they come to you and want to pray to receive the Spirit of God into their heart, here are some verses to review as well as a sample prayer to lead them through. You can't mess this up—just let the Spirit lead!

WE ARE ALL SINNERS.

"For all have sinned and come short of the glory of God," (Romans 3:23 NIV).

THE PENALTY FOR SIN IS DEATH!

"For the wages of sin is death, but the gift of God is eternal life through Jesus Christ our Lord" (Romans 6:23 KJV).

GOD'S LOVE FOR US.

"For God so loved the world that he gave His one and only Son, that whosoever believes in Him shall not perish, but have eternal life" (John 3:16 NIV).

WE MUST RECEIVE HIS FREE GIFT OF SALVATION!

"If you declare with your mouth, 'Jesus is Lord,' and believe in your heart that God raised him from the dead, you will be saved. For it is with your heart that you believe and are justified, and it is with your mouth that you profess your faith and are saved" (Romans 10:9-10 NIV).

"For whosoever shall call upon the name of the Lord shall be saved" (Romans 10:13 NIV).

EXAMPLE: PRAYER OF SALVATION

Father,

I know I have missed the mark and that I am a sinner. I believe Jesus is Your Son and that He was born of a virgin. I believe He died on the cross and shed His blood to pay for my spiritual freedom. I believe He was buried and rose to life from the grave. I ask You, Lord Jesus, to come into my heart and make me new! Change my heart and my life Lord, I want to know You! Thank You, Jesus, for the forgiveness of my sins, your gift of Salvation and everlasting life, because of Your grace and mercy! Amen.

LESSON 1

Healing with Jesus

KEY POINT

The ministry of Jesus was to bind up the brokenhearted and set captives free, all through faith and truth, which is His desire for you. This lesson biblically explains the effects of unaddressed pain and sin, how bitterness sets in, and what to do about it.

WHY THIS MATTERS

Hurt people, hurt people (Matthew 12:33-34). As long as you have a heart full of pain, you are unable to walk fully and freely in your God-given identity.

HOW TO APPLY

Often, it's hard to realize you are carrying around deep levels of hurt and pain. You will begin the healing process by learning how wounds, whether caused by choices you've made or no fault of your own, can be turned into lies, resulting in bitterness and sin.

Leader's Guide

LESSON 1

Healing with Jesus

MEMORY VERSES
Proverbs 4:23 (Write your memory verse in the space below.)

QUIET TIME VERSES
Proverbs 4:20-27; Isaiah 61:1-8; 1 Corinthians 13:4-8; James 1:2-7; John 21:25; Romans 8:18-30; John 7:37-39; Ephesians 6:10-17

Complete Lesson 1 and try to have four to seven Quiet Times before your next meeting. The verses provided above are for additional Quiet Times after you have completed this lesson. To ensure you are using the verse in the correct context, be sure to read several verses before and after the suggested Quiet Time passage(s).

KEY POINT
The ministry of Jesus was to bind up the brokenhearted and set captives free, all through faith and truth, which is His desire for you. This lesson biblically explains the effects of unaddressed pain and sin, how bitterness sets in, and what to do about it.

WHY THIS MATTERS
Hurt people, hurt people (Matthew 12:33-34). As long as you have a heart full of pain, you are unable to walk fully and freely in your God-given identity.

HOW TO APPLY
Often, it's hard to realize you are carrying around deep levels of hurt and pain. You will begin the healing process by learning how wounds, whether caused by choices you've made or no fault of your own, can be turned into lies, resulting in bitterness and sin.

Leader's Notes

- This lesson may take two weeks to complete. Remember to be mindful to begin and end on time.

- Reiterate the importance of using a concordance, dictionary, and thesaurus as part of the Quiet Time.

- Remember to encourage your group members to go slow and focus on the process, not the end result. Use additional verses from the lesson for extra Quiet Time resources as needed.

- PRAY for your group as they begin experiencing Jesus as the One who comes to bind up the brokenhearted and set the captives free. Stay true to teaching the Word and let the Holy Spirit do the hard work!

- Highlight one or two questions from the lesson to be discussed in group time, allowing each person to share an answer. For quick reference, write the page numbers of the questions you chose to discuss below.

Navigating Your Group Time

- Spend 15-20 minutes in worship.
- As the time of worship comes to a close, the leader should begin the WAR method of prayer.
- Write a quick summary of Lesson 1 in the space below. Share this with the group to begin the lesson after the time of prayer is finished.

- Ask everyone to share their "Main Take-Away" from the end of the lesson.
- Ask each person to share a Quiet Time.
- As a group, go over the two different *Heart Illustrations* on pages 11 and 14.
- Have each person share her findings from the "Words Exercise" on pages 16-17.
- Reiterate the importance of looking up the meanings of keywords on pages 17-18.
- If time allows, ask everyone to share an answer from the questions the leader highlighted (1-2 questions).
- Read sections: "Review" and "Before Your Next Lesson".
- Break into pairs and recite your verses.
- Remind everyone to sign off on each other's course record in the back of the book.

Participant's Guide

LESSON 1

Healing with Jesus

MEMORY VERSES
Proverbs 4:23 (Write your memory verse in the space below.)

QUIET TIME VERSES
Proverbs 4:20-27; Isaiah 61:1-8; 1 Corinthians 13:4-8; James 1:2-7; John 21:25; Romans 8:18-30; John 7:37-39; Ephesians 6:10-17

Complete Lesson 1 and try to have four to seven Quiet Times before your next meeting. The verses provided above are for additional Quiet Times after you have completed this lesson. To ensure you are using the verse in the correct context, be sure to read several verses before and after the suggested Quiet Time passage(s).

KEY POINT
The ministry of Jesus was to bind up the brokenhearted and set captives free, all through faith and truth, which is His desire for you. This lesson biblically explains the effects of unaddressed pain and sin, how bitterness sets in, and what to do about it.

WHY THIS MATTERS
Hurt people, hurt people (Matthew 12:33-34). As long as you have a heart full of pain, you are unable to walk fully and freely in your God-given identity.

HOW TO APPLY
Often, it's hard to realize you are carrying around deep levels of hurt and pain. You will begin the healing process by learning how wounds, whether caused by choices you've made or no fault of your own, can be turned into lies, resulting in bitterness and sin.

Participant's Notes

- Complete this lesson before your next meeting. Be sure to answer the questions marked with a 💭 and be ready to share your answers with the group. It's important to remember there are no wrong answers to the questions throughout the lessons because they are your thoughts, so be free in how you answer!

- Use the space provided in the margins to take notes, write down additional Scripture references you find, or to draw pictures that come to mind as you journey through "Healing with Jesus."

- Use a concordance, dictionary, and thesaurus as part of your Quiet Time.

- Remember to go slow and focus on the process, not the end result. True transformation is a process, not a race.

- PRAY for yourself and your fellow group members as you begin experiencing Jesus as the One who comes to bind up the brokenhearted and set the captives free.

Healing with Jesus

Layla recalled how she loved being a big sister. Her mother had told her stories of how at three years old, she was so proud of her new role. But even more than that, she loved her daddy! Layla was floored by the fact that she was once called a "daddy's girl"! At age four, her parents divorced and her dad rarely came around to see her. Somewhere along the way, Layla believed the lie that she wasn't very special, and may even be unlovable. She learned to harden her heart and not trust others easily. She learned from her step-dad that father figures just provided necessities, like food and clothing, but never cherished or delighted in her.

There were no daddy-daughter dates, long walks, or conversations. No one built her swing sets or threw her tea parties with feather boas. No man had ever invested in her character or taught her that she didn't have to settle for someone to love her.

As Layla and I talked, I suspected Layla had projected this lack of expectation onto her Heavenly Father as well. She confirmed it when I asked her if she felt Jesus loved her. Layla jokingly replied, "Well, yes the Bible and the nursery rhyme tell me so!" In essence, she believed God loved her because He had to—not because He delighted in her or because she was His cherished creation.

As an adult, Layla stuffed her failures inside, trying to hide them from God and her loved ones so that she didn't disappoint anyone. Layla believed she needed to be good and pleasing for God to love and accept her as His own. She had bought the lie that if she disappointed God, He would leave her.

This had affected how she lived as a wife, mother, friend, coworker, and most importantly, how she thought about God. Until she allowed God to come in and heal the lies that had taken root in her heart, she wasn't able to believe or experience the fullness of God's love for her.

Layla didn't want to pour into her marriage and children from a heart full of yuckiness. She wanted pure, clean truth that only comes from a loving, Heavenly Father. As Layla grew in her relationship with God, she started to trust Him with her deepest feelings. She began to tell Him of the more shameful things she had tried to hide in the past. The more Layla poured out the infection in her heart to God, the closer she felt to Him.

She learned through her time alone with God that He is always waiting and willing to listen to her for as long as she wants to talk. She came to understand that He never has more important places to go or more meaningful business to handle. She realized He is always present, and when her heart is breaking, He comes even closer. She began to see there was nothing too ugly in her heart that He wouldn't love her through, because He knew her intentions even when she was confused and felt worthless.

The more Layla poured out the infection in her heart to God, the closer she felt to Him. Layla realized she was a cherished and chosen daughter of the One True King, and she began to walk in freedom for the first time in her life. Until now, she had always had a relationship with God that she could live with, but now, she had one she could not live without!

YOU ARE IN THE HEART OF GOD

Layla would not have been able to break free from this cycle of brokenness without intimacy with Jesus. This required her to allow Him to heal her by cleaning out the layers of wounds and lies that had built up in her heart. Jesus loves you and He wants you to know it! What better way could He prove it than by binding up your heart wounds and setting you free? And, as if that wasn't enough, He traded His very life for yours in the most traumatic way. The God of all creation loves you more than anything else He spoke into existence, and His actions prove it!

Being a cherished daughter of God is not determined by your past, what kind of home you come from, your ethnicity, weight, level of education, or what you have or have not accomplished in life. When you accept Jesus as your Lord and Savior, you are adopted into the heart of God—no exceptions. Even before you were saved, the God of all creation was pursuing you, wanting to spend ever-after with you.

The importance of binding up the brokenhearted and setting the captives free is so you may be firmly planted in the Truth of your Creator, and be found with no condemnation in you, because your confidence is in God (1 John 3:21). When the enemy strikes you with lies about your Heavenly Father and about your identity, you answer with HIS truth and remain steadfast in your identity in Him.

The Word of God states in 1 John 3:20 that the contents of your heart can condemn you, but thankfully God knows the truth. "Letting the Healer Heal" is about allowing God to search out the pain in your heart by removing the lies. This can only be done through the Word and the Holy Spirit.

The purpose is to prepare the soil of your heart for good seeds waiting to be planted. If the soil in our garden is full of rocks and life-choking weeds, then the wounds soak up the nutrients, causing fruit-bearing seeds to shrivel and die before they are able to bloom. By allowing Jesus into these hurt places, He is able to clean the soil of our hearts from the hurt that keeps us from being fruitful, making our hearts a receptive and fertile field for His planting and harvest.

> THEN HE TOLD THEM MANY THINGS IN PARABLES, SAYING: "A FARMER WENT OUT TO SOW HIS SEED. AS HE WAS SCATTERING THE SEED, SOME FELL ALONG THE PATH, AND THE BIRDS CAME AND ATE IT UP. SOME FELL ON ROCKY PLACES, WHERE IT DID NOT HAVE MUCH SOIL. IT SPRANG UP QUICKLY, BECAUSE THE SOIL WAS SHALLOW. BUT WHEN THE SUN CAME UP, THE PLANTS WERE SCORCHED, AND THEY WITHERED BECAUSE THEY HAD NO ROOT. OTHER SEED FELL AMONG THORNS, WHICH GREW UP AND CHOKED THE PLANTS. STILL OTHER SEED FELL ON GOOD SOIL, WHERE IT PRODUCED A CROP—A HUNDRED, SIXTY OR THIRTY TIMES WHAT WAS SOWN.
> —MATTHEW 13:3-8 NIV

HOW DID WE GET SO FAR AWAY FROM WHO WE WERE DESIGNED TO BE?

Before claiming our rightful place in the heart of God, we embellished ourselves with the world's deceptive ideas of value, freedom, and love. We believed these lies filled in our gaps, making us whole, valuable, and worthy of affection, yet all the while we were being led further away from who God created us to be. Before we are wives, mothers, sisters, friends, or disciple-makers, we are daughters of the Most High!

Now let's just talk straight for a minute. It's a common thought and practice among believers to avoid putting focus on the enemy, and I agree! While we should never take our eyes off of Jesus to see what Satan is doing, 2 Corinthians 2:11 tells us to be aware of the enemy's schemes. The enemy, also known as *"the father of lies"* (John 8:44), revels in our pain and despair. He comes for one purpose, and that is to "steal, kill, and destroy" anything precious to God (see John 10:10).

Our "heart" is where our beliefs, attitudes, feelings, emotions, and memories are stored; it's our personality, where we store the things we value. Having unaddressed wounds, sin, painful memories, etc., in our hearts leaves the door wide open for the enemy to exploit our beliefs, attitudes, feelings, emotions, and memories. He starts by whispering lies that our young, inexperienced minds cannot navigate around.

Eventually, these lies become woven into the strands of our spiritual DNA, affecting the choices we make, such as how we treat others, and how we view ourselves and God. By giving our hurts and disappointments to God, the Father of Truth (see John 14:6), we are able to work through the details of the deception effectively, thus allowing God to bind up our broken hearts and set us free from lies (Isaiah 61:1). So let us not be like the crowd that Jesus saw, harassed and helpless, like sheep without a shepherd. We have a great and mighty Shepherd. Let us realize it and call on His Name!

> **AS WATER REFLECTS A FACE, SO A MAN'S HEART REFLECTS THE MAN.**
> **—PROVERBS 27:19 NIV84**

TAKE A MOMENT TO STUDY *THE HURTING HEART* ILLUSTRATION ON THE NEXT PAGE.

The Hurting Heart

SELF-HATRED • SHAME • GUILT • WORTHLESSNESS • ANXIETY • BITTERNESS • JEALOUSY • RAGE • ANGER • PRIDE • RESENTMENT • REVENGE • CONTROL • VIOLENCE • SICKNESS • FEAR • ADDICTION • FRUSTRATION • THOUGHTS OF SUICIDE • WORRY • ADULTERY • INSECURITY • SELF-RIGHTEOUSNESS

3 This large layer represents what happens if we choose to believe the lie. When we adopt Satan's thought patterns about ourselves in place of God's truth, we enter into a cycle of sinful nature. The pus and infection caused by the lies we believed affects how we view ourselves, how we view God, how we love our husbands, raise our children, and interact with the world. We pour into others from this layer of our heart. *(see Matthew 12:34-35)*

2 Satan exploits the wound with his lies about God and our identity. This is the moment where we choose to claim truth or believe the lies from the enemy, thus determining the contents of our hearts. *(see John 10:10)*

1 The smallest area represents the real issue/s or original entry point of the wound. This could have taken place in childhood or adulthood and may include hurtful words or actions, or any type of abuse. *(see John 16:33)*

ILLUSTRATION 2.1
Disclaimer: This illustration is an interpretative graphic of how the spiritual heart functions for the purposes of spiritual healing in *Letting the Healer Heal* by Jessie North. In no way should it be used in physical interpretations or to replace professional medical care. It's intended use is for the *Cultivating Holy Beauty* series only.

"I have told you these things, so that in me you may have peace. In this world you will have trouble. But take heart! I have overcome the world." (John 16:33 NIV84)

"The thief comes only to steal and kill and destroy; I have come that they may have life, and have it more abundantly." (John 10:10 NIV84)

"...For out of the overflow of the heart the mouth speaks. The good man brings good things out of the good stored up in him, and the evil man brings evil things out of the evil stored up in him." (Matthew 12:34b-35 NIV84)

LESSON 1 HEALING WITH JESUS

The smallest area at the bottom of the heart illustration is the wound. Countless situations can cause these wounds in us. Some examples include hurtful words spoken, being bullied, verbal, emotional, physical, spiritual, or sexual abuse, the loss of a spouse, child, parent or family member, or a cherished friend, abandonment by one or both parents, the divorce of your parents, an unfaithful spouse, a porn-addicted spouse, etc. The list goes on and on.

The next area is where Satan makes his attempt with his lies concerning the wound, like, "I am unlovable" or "I am not smart enough" or even, "If I knew how to satisfy my husband, he would not have turned to pornography."

The simple and clear truth is that the enemy hates you and me, and he is always looking for ways to steal our identity in Christ. Satan's main purpose is to get us to sin against God, causing fellowship to break between our Creator and us. As a result, we tend to hear the enemy louder than we do our Heavenly Father, and we begin to move further and further away from the truth, which brings us to the biggest section in the illustration.

The pus and sickness of layer #3 is designed to keep us from seeing the very bottom layer—the truth—instead of the lies concerning the wound. In my view, this is the portion of our spiritual heart from which we function in our day-to-day lives. It affects our ability to love God, how we function in our marriages, how we parent, and how we interact with the world. The wound is the potential entry point for Satan. If we choose not to believe the lie by saying, "No, I am not the reason my dad left the family," then Satan gains no authority in our lives because we have chosen truth over the lie he tried to plant.

However, if we choose to believe the lie, then that wound becomes infected and it continues to fester. The infection continues to spread and taints more and more of our thoughts about ourselves and God. The temptation to believe the thought is not the sin, but when we reject truth and believe the lie, we commit treason against God, giving Satan authority to harass us—by giving in to the sin.

Satan cannot gain authority in our lives unless given authority. Plainly put, when we step into the temptation of Satan and give in to sin, we give Satan authority in our lives. Remember, God tempts no one (James 1:13), but Satan is referred to as "the tempter" in Matthew 4:3.

To walk in freedom, we must allow Jesus to show us the truth, before we can get rid of the anger, hurt, and unforgiveness in our heart. Jesus is the only One who can truly heal us. It is only then that we can move forward in forgiveness and walk in freedom.

Can you walk cancer-free if you have not been healed of the cancer? No, to be cancer-free, you must be healed of the cancer; it must be taken out of your physical body. Unaddressed hurt and pain work the same way in your spiritual self. It's not just going to go away if left untreated, but will grow and fester, changing how you think and act. It will eventually steal your life, whether it be through depression, never discovering your purpose, not knowing who you were created to be in Christ, and even physical death (1 Corinthians 15:44-49; Romans 12:2, 1 Thessalonians 5:23-24).

> **Dear friend, I hope all is well with you and that you are as healthy in body as you are strong in spirit.**
> **—3 John 1:2 NLT**

Matthew 12:33-35 clearly describes the heart illustration on page 11. While having a quiet time on this passage, I went to the Strong's Concordance through **www.blueletterbible.org** and found that the Greek word used for "evil" is ponēros. This is also the same Greek word as "hurtful." It was one of those "ah-ha!" moments for me. In my experience evil is always hurtful! This is where we get the term "hurt people, hurt people." If we have unresolved pain, hatred, anger, etc., in our hearts, it is scriptural that it will flow out of our mouths and inflict pain on others. We often don't realize this is the case, which is why we need to ask Jesus to help reveal the infection to us. Though some will have deeper wounds than others, we all have hurts that we need to surrender to God. "If we claim to be without sin, we deceive ourselves and the truth is not in us" (1 John 1:8 NIV).

However, when we cling to the truth of our Living God, our hearts become full of godly thoughts, the fruit that comes from His Spirit within us. The wound is healed and erased, and as you can see from the illustration on the following page, the hard crust of our hearts softens and breaks up, allowing God's love and good seed to come in and take root in the soft and supple soil of our hearts. God's love radiates from us, as we begin to walk in our destiny as daughters of God, as wives, mothers, and disciple-makers. We help advance the kingdom on earth, powerful and effective as the fruit of our lives proves our love and hope in Jesus.

TAKE A MOMENT TO STUDY *THE HEALTHY HEART* ILLUSTRATION ON THE NEXT PAGE.

The Healthy Heart

LOVE JOY
PEACE · PATIENCE · KINDNESS
GOODNESS · FAITHFULNESS
GENTLENESS
SELF-CONTROL

> "Plant the good seeds of righteousness, and you will harvest a crop of love. Plow up the hard ground of your hearts, for now is the time to seek the LORD, that he may come and shower righteousness upon you" (Hosea 10:12 NLT).

ILLUSTRATION 2.2
Disclaimer: This illustration is an interpretative graphic of how the spiritual heart functions for the purposes of spiritual healing in *Letting the Healer Heal* by Jessie North. In no way should it be used in physical interpretations or to replace professional medical care. It's intended use is for the *Cultivating Holy Beauty* series only.

The beautiful and bright heart on page 14, filled with the things of God is where we are headed in "Letting the Healer Heal." Keeping the hard crust of our hearts broken up, as well as maintaining the quality of soil inside, is a lifelong process, a process you will learn in the next several weeks. We live in a dark and hurtful world, being subjected to new hurt and pain every day. The goal of this book is to allow Jesus to clean out any present infection in your heart and heal the wounds underneath, as well as learn how to identify the real enemy real-time and claim truth so you can maintain a healthy heart as you walk in freedom!

Read Hosea 10:12 in the illustration and apply it to what you have learned so far. Whose responsibility is it to break up the hard ground of our hearts? Write your answer below.

After reading about the heart illustrations, what comes to mind about your own heart's condition?

IT'S TIME TO DUST OFF YOUR GLOVES AND GARDENING TOOLS GIRLS. WE HAVE WORK TO DO!

Allowing Jesus to heal you is a necessary step in your spiritual journey for deeper intimacy with Him. Trust His Word and the process laid out for you. As you move through "Letting the Healer Heal", take time to look up the verses mentioned. Ask God to help your heart understand His Word and for His help dealing with any unbelief you may have (Mark 9:24).

True transformation takes time, it is encouraged to move at the pace of the group. There is no need to rush through the lessons, just make sure to stay on task. In the lessons ahead, your relationship with Jesus will be elevated to a new level as you learn how to pour out your heart to God through writing Hurt Letters.

> Go to www.CultivatingHolyBeauty.com to order a journal created specifically for *Cultivating Holy Beauty* or use your current Quiet Time journal.

Words Exercise

Sometimes we have a cultural view of what common words mean. As we enter into this place of healing and transformation with Jesus, it will be important to have a clear meaning of what certain words mean. Take the word "heart" for instance. There are over 800 references in Scripture about our hearts. It's important to understand what part of us Scripture is referring to when it says to "guard your **heart** above all else" (Proverbs 4:23-24), and that "your **heart** will condemn you" (1 John 3:20).

Another example is the prayer for us in Ephesians 3:16-17a; "I pray that out of His glorious riches he may strengthen our inner being so that Christ may dwell in your **hearts** through faith." God isn't referring to the cute little shape we doodle on our papers around the things we love, nor is He referencing the organ in our bodies that keeps our blood moving. Do you see the value in understanding what part of ourselves He is referencing when He is giving us instruction? How can we guard our hearts if we don't understand which part of our make-up He is talking about?

In the space below use your Bible concordance, like the Strong's Concordance or **www.BlueLetterBible.org** (both are available in apps for smartphones), to get a better understanding of the term "**heart**" as well as the underlined words in the verses on pages 17-18. Rewrite the verse in your own words using your findings. Be sure to note any convictions the Holy Spirit gives you during this exercise and be prepared to share with the group.

- **STEP 1**: I recommend taking your time through the word study to help you grasp the biblical meaning behind keywords in Scripture. This is vital to moving forward in healing and deeper intimacy with God.
- **STEP 2**: Using your **concordance**, look up the highlighted and underlined words, plus any others you may not fully understand in the verses below.
- **STEP 3**: Rewrite the verse in your own words using your findings from step 1 above for greater understanding.

Remember, the more you put into these exercises the more you will get out of them. God's Word never returns void!

USE THIS EXERCISE FOR YOUR QUIET TIMES THIS WEEK.

Proverbs 4:23 NIV84
"Above all else, guard your heart, for it is the wellspring of life."

Psalm 139:23-24 NIV84
"Search me, O God, and know my heart; test me and know my anxious thoughts. See if there is any offensive way in me, and lead me in the way everlasting."

1 John 3:18-20 NIV84

"Dear children, let us not love with words or tongue but with actions and in truth. This then is how we know that we belong to the truth, and how we set our hearts at rest in His presence whenever our hearts condemn us. For God is greater than our hearts, and He knows everything."

Ephesians 3:16-17a NIV84

"I pray that out of His glorious riches He may strengthen you with power through His Spirit in your inner being, so that Christ may dwell in your hearts through faith."

Matthew 12:34b-35 NIV84

". . . For out of the overflow of the heart the mouth speaks. The good man brings good things out of the good stored up in him, and the evil man brings evil things out of the evil stored up in him."

💭 Based on your findings above, what part of our being makes up our "heart"? List your thoughts and be prepared to share with the group.

Life Application

Johnny was the oldest of his siblings. He grew up with a dominant mother and absent father. He was always getting interrupted when he spoke. Johnny never felt like he was heard, and he began to believe the lie that what he had to say wasn't important. As an adult, Johnny struggled with feeling insecure about his self-worth and value. He hated to be interrupted!

One night while sitting at the dinner table with his own family, Johnny was telling a story about work when his wife, intrigued, interrupted him with a question about his story. Johnny pressed his lips together and gripped the edges of the dining table with both hands so tightly his knuckles turned white. Awkward silence fell over the table as his wife began to apologize for not waiting until he was finished to ask a question. Johnny told her to forget it and refused to tell the rest of his story, finishing his supper in silence.

In this example, Johnny's wound was that he wasn't listened to as a child. He was always spoken over and interrupted. The enemy used this to convince Johnny that his thoughts were of little importance. As he matured, he became bitter in his heart, which caused him to be harsh and unloving towards his family, causing another generation of hurt and frustrated children. Johnny was not a bad man, but as God's Word explains, *hurt people, hurt people* (see Matthew 12:33-35).

When we have unaddressed wounds, we interpret every word spoken to us through the grid of our pain, often leaving us with the emotional maturity level of the age we were when the wound happened. Frequently, hurt people live trying to fight off depression and frustration as a result of these bad seeds that were planted in their hearts somewhere along the way. Pain comes in various degrees of intensity. You may not have obvious wounds, but due to the increased darkness in our world, it's a good idea to ask God to show you if there is something He would like to heal or correct in you.

> WHEN HE SAW THE CROWDS HE HAD COMPASSION ON THEM, BECAUSE THEY WERE HARASSED AND HELPLESS, LIKE SHEEP WITHOUT A SHEPHERD.
> —MATTHEW 9:36 NIV

Experiencing God in this intimate way helps Him to become real to us. Sadly, I admit, before I encountered God in my hurt places like this, He was not as personal to me as I thought. I was learning as an adult through hearing sermons and Sunday school lessons about a loving God who did all of these amazing things. However, it wasn't until I started experiencing healing in my own heart that Jesus became someone I truly relied on in hard times.

As much as I wanted to believe He was the same today as He was in biblical times, it took experiencing His healing presence in the pain of my own life for my heart to fully believe He could love me enough to die for me. I was able to trust Him on deeper levels with less effort on my part because I had experienced His grace and love first hand. My ability to **not be afraid and just believe** (see Mark 5:36), that every word of God is flawless—and He wants good things for me, like a whole heart and freedom from the lies that once held me captive—increased after I allowed Jesus into my hurt places. I realized I didn't want a relationship with God I could live with, I wanted one I could not live without!

When I saw Jesus walk into the middle of my pain, His goodness became undeniable to my heart. Being set free from lies about myself and God gave me a more accurate view of love. I was better able to see others the way Jesus sees them—which was not as evil, but as broken and hurting.

Review

1. To understand why Jesus cared so much about binding up the brokenhearted and setting captives free, we must be able to grasp the effects of unaddressed pain and woundedness, how bitterness sets in, and what to do about it.

2. True transformation takes time and there is no need to rush through the lessons, just make sure to stay on task.

3. Remember to pray for your group mates as well as yourself! You are all headed into enemy territory that must be seized and given back to its rightful Owner, with a capital "O." Do not be unaware of the enemy's schemes and stay in the LIGHT!

4. Take time to look up every verse mentioned and ask God to help your heart understand, and to help with any unbelief you may have.

Main Take-Away

What was your main take-away from this lesson?

Before Your Next Meeting

1. Try to have a Quiet Time at least four times this week using the verses listed for Lesson 2.

2. Memorize **Luke 1:45** this week.

3. Come prepared having finished Lesson 2.

Notes

LESSON 2

Faith in the Healer

KEY POINT
Knowing God's character is vital for your spiritual healing and growth. Trusting someone with our deepest secrets and pain requires a deeper relationship. This lesson focuses on the characteristics and loving nature of God.

WHY THIS MATTERS
Knowing our Father's character is key to growing in unwavering faith and trust that He is good and the promises of His Word are meant for you.

HOW TO APPLY
Spend time meditating on the passages of Scripture provided in this lesson. As you move through the lessons to follow, come back and revisit the Scriptures on pages 33-34 for remembrance of God's goodness, love, and mercy.

Leader's Guide

LESSON 2

Faith in the Healer

MEMORY VERSES
Luke 1:45 (Write your memory verse in the space below.)

QUIET TIME VERSES
See the exercise on pages 33-34 for your Quiet Time verses.
Complete Lesson 2 and try to have four to seven Quiet Times before your next meeting. To ensure you are using the verse in the correct context, be sure to read several verses before and after the suggested Quiet Time passage(s).

KEY POINT
Knowing God's character is vital for your spiritual healing and growth. Trusting someone with our deepest secrets and pain requires a deeper relationship. This lesson focuses on the characteristics and loving nature of God.

WHY THIS MATTERS
Knowing our Father's character is key to growing in unwavering faith and trust that He is good and the promises of His Word are meant for you.

HOW TO APPLY
Spend time meditating on the passages of Scripture provided in this lesson. As you move through the lessons to follow, come back and revisit the Scriptures on pages 33-34 for remembrance of God's goodness, love, and mercy.

Leader's Notes

- This lesson may take two weeks to complete. **Remember to encourage your group members to go slow and focus on the process and not the end result.** Use additional Scripture verses from the lesson for extra Quiet Time resources as needed.

  - The exercise on pages 33-34 will provide the Quiet Time verses for this lesson.

  - Be careful to reiterate the importance of using a concordance, dictionary and thesaurus as part of their Quiet Time.

- Encourage your group members to go slow and focus on the verses about God's character.

- PRAY for your group to grasp who their Heavenly Father is through focusing on the verses in this lesson.

- Stay true to teaching the Word, letting the Holy Spirit do the hard work! Your role as the leader is to point your group members back to Jesus in the heat of their battles.

- Highlight one or two questions from the lesson to be discussed in group time, allowing each person to share an answer. For quick reference, write the page numbers of the questions you chose to discuss below.

Navigating Your Group Time

- Spend 15-20 minutes in worship.
- As the time of worship comes to a close, the leader should begin the WAR method of prayer.
- Write a quick summary of Lesson 2 in the space below. Share this with the group to begin the lesson after the time of prayer is finished

- Ask everyone to share their "Main Take-Away" from the end of the lesson.
- Have each person share a Quiet Time.
- Meditate on the verses about God's character on pages 33-34. Remind the women in the group to come back to these verses refreshing their hearts often with them.
- Sign the "Commitment of Faith" on page 38
- If time allows, have each person share an answer from the questions the leader highlighted (1-2 questions).
- Read sections: "Review" and "Before Your Next Lesson".
- Break into pairs and recite your verses. Encourage accuracy as the Word is our greatest weapon!
- Remind everyone to sign off on each other's course record in the back of the book.

Participant's Guide

LESSON 2

Faith in the Healer

MEMORY VERSES
Luke 1:45 (Write your memory verse in the space below.)

QUIET TIME VERSES
See the exercise on pages 33-34 for your Quiet Time verses.
Complete Lesson 2 and try to have four to seven Quiet Times before your next meeting. To ensure you are using the verse in the correct context, be sure to read several verses before and after the suggested Quiet Time passage(s).

KEY POINT
Knowing God's character is vital for your spiritual healing and growth. Trusting someone with our deepest secrets and pain requires a deeper relationship. This lesson focuses on the characteristics and loving nature of God.

WHY THIS MATTERS
Knowing our Father's character is key to growing in unwavering faith and trust that He is good and the promises of His Word are meant for you.

HOW TO APPLY
Spend time meditating on the passages of Scripture provided in this lesson. As you move through the lessons to follow, come back and revisit the Scriptures on pages 33-34 for remembrance of God's goodness, love, and mercy.

Participant's Notes

- The exercise on pages 33-34 will provide the Quiet Time verses for this lesson.

- This lesson may take two weeks to complete. Use additional Scripture verses from pages 33-34 for extra Quiet Time resources as needed.

- Use a concordance, dictionary and thesaurus to go deeper in your Quiet Time.

- Don't be afraid to spend as many Quiet Times as needed on the Characteristics of God exercise for greater understanding of how truly good and trustworthy God is.

- PRAY for yourself and group members to grasp who their Heavenly Father is through focusing on the verses in this lesson.

- Complete this lesson before your next meeting. Be sure to answer the questions marked with a 💬 and be ready to share your answers with the group. It's important to remember there are no wrong answers to the questions throughout the lessons because they are your thoughts, so be free in how you answer!

- Use the space provided in the margins to take notes, write down additional Scripture references you find or to draw pictures that come to mind as you journey through "Faith in the Healer."

Faith in the Healer

When I was a little girl, I wanted to believe I had been created for more than just going through the motions of an earthly life. But because I didn't know Scripture, I was unaware of God's plans for me. As I entered my teens, the void became more obvious and more painful, but I still did not know how to fill it. As I bumbled around in the darkness, I ended up going down spiritual dead-end roads that left me blind, empty, and spiritually starving. I was like the crowd Jesus talked about in Matthew 9:36, "harassed and helpless, like a sheep without a shepherd." Looking back over my life now, God's hand has been undeniable every step of the way as He led me out of the desert. It is only because of His pursuit of me that I am able to write to you today.

God knew how ill-equipped I was to write the series of books titled, *Cultivating Holy Beauty*. Because of the mistakes I made in the past, I never dreamed God would want to use my life for His kingdom work and glory. I tried to write off His call on my life as "wishful thinking" on my part. When the burden did not lift, I reminded God of my inadequacies over and over; however, it did not seem to faze Him. I asked Him, "Why would you want someone like me, God?" He answered, "Because I created you for a purpose, and because of your desire to be obedient. You believe Me when I speak to you through My Word and through My Spirit."

All my life I craved something deeper and I found it when I found my identity in Jesus. I chose to believe Proverbs 30:5, "Every Word of God is flawless; He is a shield to those who take refuge in Him." This is truly the verse that did it for me. When I realized Jesus was everything I was searching for, I dove in, completely surrendering to the Word and the guidance of His Holy Spirit. For more than ten years I had a relationship with God that I could live with—it was comfortable but powerless, bringing about zero transformation in my life. However, when I fully surrendered to the truth, that "every Word of God is flawless," I discovered a relationship with Jesus I could not live without—the kind of relationship that would carry me out of darkness and through the rough waters life would bring.

Through my surrender, God began to bind up my broken places and set me free from the captivity of lies I had believed for so long. It no longer mattered if I thought I wasn't able, or if others thought I was incapable of what God had called me to. It no longer mattered if other people approved of me or thought my love for Jesus was extreme. I was sold out to Jesus, once and for all. I believed in the Scriptures and the power of God, and even with all of my weaknesses, He would be GLORIFIED.

I had never seen love, hope, and power like His in the other places I had looked as a teen. The only place I purpose to fall now is deeper in love with my Creator as I learn more about God the Father—my precious loving Father in Heaven, Jesus my Hero—the Living Word, and the Holy Spirit—my ever-present Help and Comforter. As God began to heal my broken heart, I was able to turn from sin that had held me captive for so long. I found joy in giving up the things the world said I needed. I discovered the honor and beauty in laying my life down for my marriage and children. My marriage began to heal, and I was learning what it truly meant to be a mother to the children God had placed in my care.

FATHER, SON, AND HOLY SPIRIT

Many great studies are available to help you get a better grasp on God the Father, God the Son and God the Holy Spirit. Or, you can do as I did and ask Him yourself! A list of key names, characteristics, and attributes of God with verses is attached on page 33 and following. Whether the attribute was manifested through the Father, the Son, or the Holy Spirit is not the focus, as all Three of those Entities are of the same divine essence. The goal is to become more familiar with the nature of God as you move through "Letting the Healer Heal".

Knowing the character of God as you journey through this book will be a vital part of the success of the healing process. Allowing God into your broken places will require you to be a woman of great faith as Mary was. Can you imagine what it must have been like to be Mary . . . a lowly servant girl who had heard from an angel of the LORD that she was miraculously pregnant with the "Son of the Most High?!"

> Think of Mary in her first trimester. Try to imagine the faith and courage it must have taken to believe what the angel of the LORD had said to her with months of no bulging baby belly or fluttering kicks from inside her womb for proof. Write down any thoughts you have.

💭 Think about how elated Mary must have been to see the fruit of her faith manifest as the Baby grew beneath her very eyes! Write down any thoughts you have.

💭 Along with the joy the physical proof of her miraculous pregnancy must have brought her, I'm certain it was also accompanied with great sorrow as her sanity was likely questioned by Joseph, her family, and friends (Matthew 1:18), when she explained what the angel of the LORD had said to her. Imagine being in Mary's shoes. Share your thoughts here.

💭 Luke 1:45 declares, "Blessed is she who has believed that what the LORD has said to her will be accomplished!" (NIV84). Mary was blessed by God because she believed what she had *heard* from Him. In a world full of darkness and ungodly influences, do you see the importance of really KNOWING the character of your heavenly Father so that you can identify when He is speaking—versus someone else? Explain your answer.

💬 How might becoming more knowledgeable on what the Bible says about the character of the Father, Son, and Holy Spirit help you grow in your faith and trust in God?

💬 What is the difference between faith and trust? Why are they both required for an effective Christian walk? (Use a dictionary for help distinguishing between the two words.)

Ladies, it's time to join the ranks of women of unwavering faith and trust like Mary! As you continue to grow in your trust of the Word and faith of how much God loves you, I pray you begin to walk with greater health and freedom. The promises of Scripture are for you! Surrender to the Holy Spirit as you journey through "Letting the Healer Heal." Let Him be your guide.

I encourage you to put your eyes intently on every verse mentioned and let it touch your heart through a Quiet Time. Knowing God's character will be imperative to recall when the battle is raging in your mind. The enemy doesn't want to lose whatever grip he has on you, so count on a fight! However, knowing verses like "He who is in you is greater than he who is in the world" (1 John 4:4 NKJV), and "What then shall we say to these things? If God is for us, who can be against us?" (Romans 8:31 MEV), will help you cling to truth and fight your way out of the quicksand and onto new solid ground!

Quiet Time Exercise

Read through the characteristics of God listed below. Highlight the characteristics that you struggle with the most. "Trina" from the upcoming Life Application story would have highlighted "He is your Father" because that was the area she struggled in the most. Once you have highlighted the characteristics, choose four to seven verses from those categories to have your Quiet Times on this week.

NAMES, ATTRIBUTES, AND CHARACTERISTICS OF YOUR HEAVENLY FATHER

- He is your **Father**: Romans 8:15-16; 1 John 3:1; Luke 12:32

- He is your **Savior**: Titus 3:5-6; Isaiah 61:1; Hebrews 7:25; 1 John 4:10-14; John 19:30

- He is your **Comforter**: Isaiah 51:12; Isaiah 41:10; 2 Corinthians 1:3-5; Psalm 23:4

- He is your **Peace**: Colossians 3:15; Galatians 5:22; Philippians 4:7; Isaiah 26:3

- He is your **Healer**: Exodus 15:25-26; Psalm 30:2; Psalm 103:2-3; Psalm 107:20; Proverbs 4:20-22; Jeremiah 17:14; Matthew 4:23-24; Matthew 8:16-17

- He is your **Strength**: Psalm 55:22; Isaiah 40:29; 41:10

- He is your **Everything**: Philippians 4:19; Mark 11:24; 2 Corinthians 9:8

- He is your **Confidence**: Psalm 16:8; Exodus 6:6

- He is **Love**: Jeremiah 31:3; Proverbs 8:17; 1 John 4:7-19; 1 Corinthians 13:13

- He is your **Worth**: Genesis 1:27; Romans 5:8; 1 Peter 1:18-19

- He is your **Protector**: Ephesians 6:10-17; 2 Thessalonians 3:3; 2 Samuel 22:3-4; 2 Timothy 4:18

- He is your **Provider**: Luke 12:32; 2 Peter 1:3; Matthew 6:31-33

- He **DEFEATED Death**: Romans 6:9; Luke 24:6-7; Romans 1:4; John 11:25; 1 Corinthians 15:55-57

- He is **Faithful**: Revelation 19:11-13; 1 Thessalonians 5:24; 2 Timothy 2:13
- He is **Trustworthy**: Numbers 23:19; 2 Samuel 7:28; 1 Timothy 1:15
- He is **Forgiving**: Nehemiah 9:17; Colossians 3:13; Ephesians 4:31-32
- He **Never Leaves you**: Romans 8:11; Deuteronomy 31:6&8; Isaiah 54:10; Joshua 1:9
- He is **Eternal**: Revelation 1:8; 1 Timothy 1:17
- He **Never Changes**: James 1:17; Hebrews 13:8; Malachi 3:6
- He is **ALL-Knowing**: John 14:26-27; 1 John 3:20; Isaiah 40:28
- He is **Omnipresent**: Jeremiah 23:24,; Acts 17:28
- He is **ALL-Powerful**: Psalm 147:5; Psalm 8:3-4; 1 Chronicles 29:12
- He **Cares**: Psalm 56:8; Hebrew 2:6-7
- He is **Merciful**: Jeremiah 3:12; Numbers 14:18a
- He is **Sympathetic**: the God of the broken-hearted: Romans 12:15; Psalm 34:18
- He is **Gentle**: Matthew 11:29; 2 Corinthians 10:1; James 3:17; Isaiah 40:11
- He **Keeps His Promises**: Numbers 23:19; 2 Timothy 2:13
- He **Fights for You**: Exodus 14:14; Deuteronomy 20:4; 2 Chronicles 20:17
- He **Left Heaven for You**: John 3:13; John 6:38; Philippians 2:5-8
- He **Gave His Very Life for you**: Romans 5:8; 1 Peter 1:18-19; Romans 6:23
- He is **Always on Time**: Luke 24:44; Ecclesiastes 3:1-8; Galatians 4:4; Psalm 31:15a
- He is **Patient**: Numbers 14:18a; Deuteronomy 8:2; Psalm 78:38
- He is **Understanding**: Isaiah 11:2; Matthew 19:26; Isaiah 40:28; Psalm 145:3
- He is **Slow to Anger**: Psalm 145:8; James 1:19; Numbers 14:18; Exodus 34:6
- He is **Kind**: Jeremiah 9:24; Titus 3:4-6; Psalm 36:7; Psalm 63:3
- He is **Compassionate**: Psalm 116:5; Psalm 103:8; Exodus 33:19
- He is **Present**: Hebrews 13:5b; Joshua 1:9

Life Application

WHY KNOWING GOD'S CHARACTER IS VITAL!

Trina grew up in a broken home. Through the course of her growing up years, she had four step dads. She experienced all different kinds of hurt and pain through her mother's marriages. It was hard for Trina to wrap her mind around what a "loving heavenly Father" might be like, when she had never experienced that from any of her earthly dads. Trina thought when she messed up, God was ashamed of her, and would leave just like her biological father had. It wasn't until she learned to have a Quiet Time that she started to perceive the Father's love for her through the verses she had been prescribed. After hundreds of Quiet Times, Trina became convinced of her heavenly Father's role as her "Abba Father." When she allowed Him to fill this role, she was able to extend forgiveness to her earthly dads for what they couldn't give her emotionally, mentally and physically, and she found great confidence and freedom in the Lord.

💬 Read through the "Names, Attributes, and Characteristics of Your heavenly Father" on pages 33-34. Like Trina, are there any that you struggle with? If so, list them here.

💬 If you responded to the question above, ask God to help you understand this part of His nature. You can also open your Internet browser and search for verses that support whatever characteristic of God you are struggling with. Look up the verses your Internet browser finds and start to learn what the Bible says about that *characteristic* of God. Write any additional verses you find in the space provided for future Quiet Time references.

LESSON 2   FAITH IN THE HEALER

💬 How might knowing God's character help you be victorious in the ways you see yourself?

ALL-POWERFUL GOD

God is All-Powerful and Will NEVER Be Defeated,

Because the Battle has Already Been Won!

Jesus CONQUERED Death When He Arose from the Grave!

Through HIS Wounds

Your Ransom was Paid!

You are No Longer a Prisoner of War!

You Must Now Learn to Live as a Free Child of THE GREAT I AM!

The Same POWER-FILLED Holy Spirit

that Resurrected Jesus from the Grave

is the Same Spirit that is Alive in You Right Now!

> HE WHO IS IN YOU IS GREATER THAN HE
> WHO IS IN THE WORLD.
> —1 JOHN 4:4 NKJV

THE BATTLE FOR YOUR FREEDOM

We all have battles in our lives to some degree. Sometimes the battles seem small. Other times they seem all-consuming as they pull you down, draining your life, hope, and energy. An invisible battle is always going on for your freedom and you are the key player through the choices you make. Holding on to Truth (The Word) and maintaining your belief in the character of God amidst the battle is your greatest weapon! You must know His character! The enemy will tempt you with lies like, "You are outnumbered," "You are alone," "This is pointless," "You don't hear from God," "Did God really say that?" and maybe even, "You aren't worth all this work!" If you hear any of these lies (or others like them) throughout this journey, know this: You are normal! Immediately then, stop what you are doing and reread "All-Powerful God". It is up to you to claim Truth in those moments! We will learn how to quickly identify lies and take thoughts captive later in the book, but for now our focus is knowing God's character so we have a firm foundation to stand on.

> When you find yourself feeling tempted to believe lies like the ones listed above, come back to this lesson. Claim the truth written previously in "All-Powerful God" as you put on the whole armor of God! Pick up the shield of faith in all circumstances, snuffing out lies of the enemy!

THE ARMOR OF GOD—EPHESIANS 6:10-18 ESV

[10] Finally, be strong in the Lord and in the strength of his might. [11] Put on the whole armor of God, that you may be able to stand against the schemes of the devil. [12] For we do not wrestle against flesh and blood, but against the rulers, against the authorities, against the cosmic powers over this present darkness, against the spiritual forces of evil in the heavenly places. [13] Therefore take up the whole armor of God, that you may be able to withstand in the evil day, and having done all, to stand firm. [14] Stand therefore, having fastened on the belt of truth, and having put on the breastplate of righteousness, [15] and, as shoes for your feet, having put on the readiness given by the gospel of peace. [16] In all circumstances take up the shield of faith, with which you can extinguish all the flaming darts of the evil one; [17] and take the helmet of salvation, and the sword of the Spirit, which is the word of God, [18] praying at all times in the Spirit, with all prayer and supplication. To that end, keep alert with all perseverance . . .

Commitment of Faith in the Healer

Faith is believing without seeing, as described in Hebrews 11:1. Not needing to see signs, miracles, and wonders to believe that Jesus is the only begotten Son of God—born of a virgin—is actual faith (Matthew 12:39; John 3:16). When you find yourself wanting to quit because you think Jesus wouldn't care to bind up your broken heart or write you a love letter, or because spiritual and emotional wound care can be just as painful, if not more, than physical wound care, take a break from the lesson and come back to this page. Read over your commitment to God and look up some of the verses listed on the previous pages. Preach the gospel to yourself over and over until you remember Jesus had you on His mind as He gave His life and defeated your darkness! The battle has already been won. Now it is time to learn how to step into victory!

> **FAITH AND FEAR BOTH BEGIN IN THE SAME PLACE; THEY ARE THE BELIEF IN SOMETHING THAT HAS NOT YET HAPPENED.**

COMMITMENT OF FAITH

Read over the commitment below and, if you agree, sign your name.

1. I acknowledge that the Spirit living in me is the same Spirit that raised Jesus Christ from the dead.

2. I agree to keep clinging to Truth when I want to quit.

3. I agree to let my sisters hold me accountable and encourage me when I feel overwhelmed.

4. I will reach out to my sisters when I feel isolated and alone.

5. I believe Jesus died for my sins and when I sincerely ask for forgiveness, He forgives me.

6. I will be courageous, trusting God's Word, and the guidance of His Spirit as He leads me to greater freedom in Jesus Christ.

7. The Holy Spirit is your accountability partner and will be with you every step of the way! He is always present and available!

Your Signature_____

Date_____

My accountability partner: Holy Spirit

Review

1. The only way to defeat the lies that plague you is by knowing Truth!

2. Know your Father's character. This is your first and best defense!

3. In every situation that comes your way, as you journey through *Cultivating Holy Beauty*, trust the Bible and keep faith in your heavenly Father's character!

Main Take-Away

What was your main take-away from this lesson?

Before Your Next Meeting

1. Try to have a Quiet Time at least four times this week using the verses listed for Lesson 3.

2. Memorize **James 1:2-4** this week.

3. Come prepared, having finished Lesson 3.

Notes

LESSON 3

The Purge

KEY POINT

Knowing God's character is vital for your spiritual healing and sharing the unsavory things we try to hide in our hearts with God is not only an act of courage and faith—but obedience. God wants to know us intimately. He tells us to pour out our hearts to Him throughout Scripture. As we learn to trust Him with our deep pain and disappointments, we begin to depend on Him in greater ways, turning to Him first for our security, worth, and value. To walk in freedom, you must first be healed from the wound.

WHY THIS MATTERS

This is important because before we can walk fully in our God-given design, we must purge the junk from our hearts that wasn't designed to be there. Jesus wants to know us. He wants us to know Him so well, that we don't hesitate before we run to Him with our pain and failures.

HOW TO APPLY

We learn to open up the places in our hearts that we have tried to hide from Jesus by asking Him where He wants to start. Then we write Jesus a detailed "Hurt Letter" about the instance that He brought to our mind.

Leader's Guide

LESSON 3

The Purge

MEMORY VERSES

James 1:2-4 (Write your memory verse in the space below.)

QUIET TIME VERSES

James 1:1-8; Luke 5:31-32; Romans 8:38-39; 1 John 1:8-10; John 16:29-33; Matthew 11:29-30; Psalm 46:1-7

Complete Lesson 3 and try to have four to seven Quiet Times before your next meeting. The verses provided above are for additional Quiet Times after you have completed this lesson. To ensure you are using the verse in the correct context, be sure to read several verses before and after the suggested Quiet Time passage(s).

KEY POINT

Knowing God's character is vital for your spiritual healing and sharing the unsavory things we try to hide in our hearts with God is not only an act of courage and faith—but obedience. God wants to know us intimately. He tells us to pour out our hearts to Him throughout Scripture. As we learn to trust Him with our deep pain and disappointments, we begin to depend on Him in greater ways, turning to Him first for our security, worth, and value. To walk in freedom, you must first be healed from the wound.

WHY THIS MATTERS

This is important because before we can walk into our God-given design, we must purge the junk from our hearts that wasn't designed to be there. Jesus wants to know us. He wants us to know Him so well, that we don't hesitate before we run to Him with our pain and failures.

HOW TO APPLY

We learn to open up the places in our hearts that we have tried to hide from Jesus by asking Him where He wants to start. Then we write Jesus a detailed "Hurt Letter" about the instance that He brought to our mind.

Leader's Notes

- This lesson may take two weeks to complete. If a group member has to miss, causing the group to sit longer than 2 weeks in a lesson, find a time to meet with her one-on-one or over the phone so the group can keep moving forward.

- PRAY for your group throughout the weeks! Spiritual warfare is real, and freedom from captivity of lies is the last thing the enemy wants for the women under your care.

- Remember it is important for the leader to set an example in transparency and vulnerability. Don't expect your group members to be vulnerable, if you aren't. Sharing your own failures makes you relatable and can give others hope.

- Sharing what you've learned through your Hurt Letters is optional. While it is good to encourage the group to share what they have been learning in their hurt letters, it is not required.

- Highlight one or two questions from the lesson to be discussed in group time, allowing each person to share an answer. For quick reference, write the page numbers of the questions you chose to discuss below.

Navigating Your Group Time

- Spend 15-20 minutes in worship.

- As the time of worship comes to a close, the leader should begin the WAR method of prayer.

- Write a quick summary of Lesson 3 in the space below. Share this with the group to begin the lesson after the time of prayer is finished

- Ask everyone to share their "Main Take-Away" from the end of the lesson.

- Have each person share a Quiet Time.

- Take time to ask and answer questions about Hurt Letters and the cleansing process. If you don't know the answer, let them know you will try to find out. Feel free to email us for help at hello@CultivatingHolyBeauty.com.

- Ask each person to share an answer from the Word study on pages 56-59.

- Remember the Confidentiality Agreement that was signed in Book 1. Remind the group members to hold anything shared in confidence!

- Although it is not required, encourage everyone to read their Hurt Letters to the group. Encourage their unhindered conversations with God. This is important in the healing and cleansing process.

- The "Helpful Scriptures" section on pages 62-63, is provided for added clarity and support of the importance of being known by God and pouring out your heart to Him.

- If time allows have each person share an answer from the questions the leader highlighted (1-2 questions).

- Read sections: "Review" and "Before Your Next Lesson".

- Break into pairs and recite your verses.

- Remind everyone to sign off on each other's course record in the back of the book.

Participant's Guide

LESSON 3

The Purge

MEMORY VERSES
James 1:2-4 (Write your memory verse in the space below.)

QUIET TIME VERSES
James 1:1-8; Luke 5:31-32; Romans 8:38-39; 1 John 1:8-10; John 16:29-33; Matthew 11:29-30; Psalm 46:1-7

Complete Lesson 3 and try to have four to seven Quiet Times before your next meeting. The verses provided above are for additional Quiet Times after you have completed this lesson. To ensure you are using the verse in the correct context, be sure to read several verses before and after the suggested Quiet Time passage(s).

KEY POINT
Knowing God's character is vital for your spiritual healing and sharing the unsavory things we try to hide in our hearts with God is not only an act of courage and faith—but obedience. God wants to know us intimately. He tells us to pour out our hearts to Him throughout Scripture. As we learn to trust Him with our deep pain and disappointments, we begin to depend on Him in greater ways, turning to Him first for our security, worth, and value. To walk in freedom, you must first be healed from the wound.

WHY THIS MATTERS
This is important because before we can walk into our God-given design, we must purge the junk from our hearts that wasn't designed to be there. Jesus wants to know us. He wants us to know Him so well, that we don't hesitate before we run to Him with our pain and failures.

HOW TO APPLY

We learn to open up the places in our hearts that we have tried to hide from Jesus by asking Him where He wants to start. Then we write Jesus a detailed "Hurt Letter" about the instance that He brought to our mind.

Participant's Notes

- This week, as you work through the lesson, PRAY for yourself and your fellow group members! Spiritual warfare is real, and freedom from captivity of lies is the last thing the enemy wants for you and your fellow group members.

- Complete this lesson before your next meeting. Be sure to answer the questions marked with a 💬 and be ready to share your answers with the group. It's important to remember there are no wrong answers to the questions throughout the lessons because they are your thoughts, so be free in how you answer!

- Use the space provided in the margins to take notes, write down additional Scripture references you find or to draw pictures that come to mind as you begin "The Purge." This is a vital part of the journey.

- Consider going into this lesson with an open heart to try something new with God. This is the beginning of rewriting the lies that have plagued you and held you captive, with God's life-giving and chain-breaking truth!

- Hurt Letters can be filled with your deepest hurts and failures, and you are not required to share them with the group. However, being vulnerable and transparent with your group members can bring healing and freedom to your heart and those you share with as well! You never know what the person beside you is struggling with. When you let down your guard and share, you make it a safer place for her to be vulnerable as well!

- Hurt Letters are a response from your heart to a caring Father. Like in worship, be free with Him in how you respond! He doesn't just want the good and pleasing parts of you—He wants all of you! Honor Him with your honesty and He will bless you for it.

- Don't worry if the Hurt Letter doesn't come right away. Just keep making your heart available to God, and the hurts will bubble to the surface when the time is right.

- The time of worship during the group meeting is provided for you to come fully present before the Lord, especially if you have had a busy day. There is not a wrong way to worship Jesus—whether you sit quietly, lay on the floor, dance, kneel, or raise your arms. This is a safe place for you to give thanks for all He has done for you—in whatever form it looks like!

Hurt Letters to God

Kendra felt like she was struggling in every area of her life. It was so hard to keep pretending all was well when this chasm kept growing inside her. She desperately wanted to break free from it, but she didn't know how. She didn't even know what "*it*" was. Kendra hoped that a committed relationship to her church might help but it was still getting worse. Her marriage had hit an all-time low when she caught her husband viewing pornography again. She felt inadequate, unattractive . . . unlovable. She often wondered where the spunky, confident girl had gone that once looked back at her in the mirror. Now she felt as though she just looked tired and sad, and she could barely look herself in the eyes. Sitting at her desk, she rummaged through her drawer looking for something to write on. Pulling out a half-used note pad, she flipped to a clean sheet and started writing frantically as though her feelings were forcing their way through the walls she had stuffed them behind.

God,

    Where am I? Where have I gone? I can't even feel anymore. My heart feels like a wasteland—cracked and parched. I'm tired of always hurting, God. I'm angry and I don't know how to get back to good. I need your help! I'm afraid my pain is going to completely consume me if I don't do something, but I don't know what to do—I don't know where to start! The pain and rejection I feel after catching him watching porn again is like the final nail in my coffin. Now my own thoughts are waging war against me! I feel like my husband has already checked out of our marriage. He has rejected me over and over by choosing to look at other women. What about our children?! What about me?! What do those girls have that I don't, besides a perfect body?! Mine is far from that!

    I am here Lord, barely . . . but I am here. At the bottom of my pain, in this black void of loneliness and eerie silence, I'm starting with You, because I have nowhere else to turn. God if I don't do this now, I'm afraid my heart will be too hardened to repair! Please don't let me go! Can I get too broken for You to fix? I'm afraid I am close. I'm bitter and disgusted by my husband's choices. I hate what he is doing to me! I hate how this feels. Father, I'm tired of disappointment and I'm tired of the only confirmation that I get from him over and over is that I am not enough for him! He continues to choose women on websites over me! Why doesn't he care about me,

God?! Why doesn't he ever choose me? Once upon a time I could hold on to hope in the face of despair, but it just keeps happening over and over and over, and I've lost my grip. I can't do it anymore . . . I'm exhausted. Please catch me Father! I can't keep putting my heart out there for him to keep breaking it! He has lost jobs and relationships because of this addiction! We've tried everything, and he keeps choosing this darkness. I feel alienated and alone, like I can't talk to anyone! Am I the only wife that fails her husband this much? I am tired, Father. I'm just tired and sad—deeply sad and really angry! If I'm honest, I think I'm a little mad at You, too, for allowing this to happen to me! I just feel isolated and hurt by everyone.

Oh Father, I'm sorry . . . The tears are flowing now. It's been a while since I've been able to cry. I'm just numb. You have known this though, haven't You? That's why You are here now, because my heart is broken. I feel You, as close as skin is to bone. I'm sorry, my anger isn't directed at You. I know You will help me find truth. Help me sort out my heart—lead me, Father. I know You love me. I know You didn't want this for me. I'm just confused and want things to get better. I just want to be enough for my husband. You are my husband tonight Lord! I will rest in Your consistent love and peace. I can trust my heart and feelings with You. I know You aren't going to leave me. Thank You for being all I need, and for reminding me that I wasn't designed to fully satisfy all of my husband's needs—only You can do that. Thank You for allowing me to come to You in my hurt and anger—for not just wanting the good parts of me, but loving the prickly and broken parts also. Please search my heart and help me change where I fall short of what You have for me.

Give me the strength to fight against the lies that wage war in my mind every day. Help me not to condemn myself or my husband. Father, please help me to see him the way You see him. Even better, right now, help me to see me the way You see me—because I don't feel loved or valued. I feel disposable.

Love,

Me

> **TRUST IN HIM AT ALL TIMES, YOU PEOPLE; POUR OUT YOUR HEARTS TO HIM, FOR GOD IS OUR REFUGE.**
> **—PSALM 62:8 NIV**

CLEANING OUT THE WEEDS

In Matthew 12, Jesus spoke a parable about a tree and its fruit. Later in the passage, Jesus explains what He means: Basically, you live from the contents in your heart. Put good things in your heart and good things will come out; put bad things in, and bad things will come out. For example, if you grew up hearing or feeling like you weren't good enough, or experienced those feelings later in a relationship, then you will most likely struggle with feelings of inadequacy and worthlessness now. Whether the lie was planted directly or indirectly, this false belief about who you are gets woven into your identity, effectively changing how you were designed to think about yourself as a cherished and chosen daughter of God. When this happens, you then enter friendships, marriage, and raising your children from the poisonous fruit grown from this bad seed.

Maybe this rotten fruit—what we'll call an infection of the heart—is a result of bad choices made in the past. Perhaps you had absolutely no control over how and why the lies were being planted in you. The good news is, either way, it can be cleaned out by giving it to God and then asking Him to fill that space with the light of Truth. If you have a spiritually healthy heart, you will have spiritually healthy fruit to prove it in your relationships with God, your marriage, and with your children.

When I was a little girl, I had a dog that I considered my best friend. We would play in the woods, cuddle on my bed, and she would run beside me while I rode my horse. Except for the company of this little dog and my horse, I always *felt* like I didn't have a lot of friends. It made me feel better to tell everyone that I was a "loner" rather than admit that I just really felt alone. Either way, I had labeled myself as someone who liked to be alone. One day my dog was run over on our property right in front of me. After she was hit, she took off running—away from me. I found her dead a few hours later after I crawled up under a house that was on the property . . . I was only 11 years old.

As I was writing this lesson, God brought this memory back to me. I felt like He said, "You used to do this same thing little daughter, when you would get hurt, instead of running to Me, you would run away, letting the lies take root in you, choking out the life you had inside." I learned that, because I ran away from refuge instead of running toward it, those hurts were never healed (see Proverbs 18:10). They were left to fester and they became prime real-estate for the enemy to plant lying seeds of loneliness, worthlessness, self-hate, shame, guilt . . .

Do you see how this works? You don't have to come from an abusive background to be wounded—to be a sitting duck for the enemy. Satan can take the most innocent moments and plant a nasty seed that completely changes the way you see yourself and God, leaving you with bitter roots and rotten fruit. This is why it's important to give these hurts to God. Your story may be completely different from the one shared in this lesson. You may have grown up in a good Christian home with parents who had a healthy relationship with God, which you benefited from. That doesn't mean you haven't adopted ungodly concepts about God's standards for yourself as His daughter. Trust the process and be willing to allow God to show you the parts in your heart He wants to heal.

Surely all of us can admit we have been wounded in this world to some degree. All of us need the healing power of God to be truly set free.

THE LETTER

It was God's idea to communicate through writing. His Word, which He breathed thousands of years ago, is still the very Word that lights our path and leads us out of darkness today. While pouring out your heart to God in this way may be new to you, there are several key people who modeled this for us in Scripture. I literally shouted with excitement when I recognized God had led David to do this in some of his letters to God in the Psalms. One of the most valuable lessons we can learn from the Book of Psalms is how to communicate with God.

The point of this next step of the journey is to grow deeper in our dependence on God, walking in greater freedom by growing closer to Him. He encourages us over and over throughout Scripture to be honest with Him, to pour out our hearts to Him, and confess our wrongdoing. We need the guidance of our heavenly Father to help us decipher the truth in the pain, anger, and sin we have held onto for so long. Sometimes it takes getting messy before God and allowing Him to help us get all the junk out so that we can actually identify the truth.

Writing Hurt Letters to God is like writing a prayer. Through Quiet Times and becoming a woman of the Word, you are learning to trust Jesus more and more. One thing I hope you grow to appreciate about God through this exercise is that you can be real with Him. This is not a time to worry about clear handwriting, punctuation, and proper grammar. This letter is just between you and God. The most important key is to trust Him and be real! Remember, God already knows everything in your heart—you can't surprise Him, shock Him, or disappoint Him.

Although God is all-knowing, He still tells us to pour out our hearts and confess our sins to Him over and over, not so He can judge or condemn us, but so He can set us free from our pain and iniquity.

Right Heart Attitudes

WHAT IF I'M SCARED TO TELL GOD THE TRUTH? WHAT IF I'M ANGRY WITH HIM?

While we must not forget that God is sovereignly supreme in every way, we also need to remember that a facet of His sovereignty includes Him being our heavenly Father. God values relationships more than He values anything else. His First and Second Commandments illustrate this.

Based on what I have learned through spending time alone with God in His Word, I believe that God understands our hearts and our yearning to be set free. I believe that in this place of learning and healing from wrong thought patterns and beliefs due to past wounds, God is aware of our misconceptions, and He takes on a gentle and patient posture with us as we search for Him while in this place.

> **GOD VALUES RELATIONSHIPS MORE THAN ANYTHING ELSE.**

> YOU DO NOT DELIGHT IN SACRIFICE, OR I WOULD BRING IT;
> YOU DO NOT TAKE PLEASURE IN BURNT OFFERINGS.
> MY SACRIFICE, O GOD, IS A BROKEN SPIRIT; A BROKEN
> AND CONTRITE HEART, GOD, YOU WILL NOT DESPISE.
> —PSALM 51:16-17 NIV84

Ephesians 4:26 reminds us not to sin in our anger. This verse clearly tells us that being angry is not a sin. Rather, it is what we do with that anger that matters. Being angry with God is more about our lack of understanding of who He is, as well as our inability to trust Him. Consider what Romans 8:28 tells us: "We know that in all things God works for the good of those who love Him . . ." (see also 2 Corinthians 4:17). This helps us recognize that God is not our enemy. He is our Savior and will work all things together for the good of those, like you and me, who love Him. This is true especially when we don't understand the situation or can't see the purpose, as in the death of a loved one or the betrayal of your husband. God wants our vulnerability—He is worthy of it! Learning to lean on Him more than we lean on anyone else is the goal. Unchecked hurt feelings are a playground for the enemy! We will cover repentance and forgiveness in Lesson 4.

> **SO HUMBLE YOURSELVES BEFORE GOD. RESIST THE DEVIL, AND HE WILL FLEE FROM YOU. COME CLOSE TO GOD, AND GOD WILL COME CLOSE TO YOU. WASH YOUR HANDS, YOU SINNERS; PURIFY YOUR HEARTS, FOR YOUR LOYALTY IS DIVIDED BETWEEN GOD AND THE WORLD. LET THERE BE TEARS FOR WHAT YOU HAVE DONE. LET THERE BE SORROW AND DEEP GRIEF. LET THERE BE SADNESS INSTEAD OF LAUGHTER, AND GLOOM INSTEAD OF JOY. HUMBLE YOURSELVES BEFORE THE LORD, AND HE WILL LIFT YOU UP IN HONOR.**
> **—JAMES 4:7-10 NLT**

If we hold on to anger and do not talk to God about it, we in fact prove we don't trust Him, and are sinning against God in our anger. Remember that God is our perfect and loving Father, and we are His beloved children. If you are still unsure about writing these letters to God, ask Him what He wants you to do with the hurt and disappointment you have inside. After all, writing is only one way of communicating with Him.

> **NO ONE WHO TRUSTS GOD LIKE THIS**
> **—HEART AND SOUL—**
> **WILL EVER REGRET IT.**
> **—ROMANS 10:11 MSG**

◯ Read two of David's Hurt Letters to God in Psalms 41 and 55. Share your thoughts.

◯ In light of Psalm 62:8 and Lamentations 2:19, I believe God waits for us to come to Him in this way. He wants us to seek Him for freedom from the chains of our past and present. How do you feel about cleaning out your heart in a Hurt Letter to God?

In the next exercise are some key truths to understand as we continue on this journey. It's important to understand the right "heart attitude" as we learn to come to God in this vulnerable way, laying ourselves bare before our Savior.

- **Step 1:** Using your concordance, look up the highlighted words, plus any others you may not fully understand in the verses below.
- **Step 2:** Rewrite the verses in your own words using your findings from Step 1 above for greater understanding.

Remember: the more you put into these exercises the more you will benefit. God's Word never returns void! Highlight your favorite discovery in this exercise and share it with your group at the next meeting.

YOUR FAITH IS ONLY AS RELIABLE AS YOUR CERTAINTY OF GOD'S LOVE FOR YOU.

Philippians 4:6-7 NIV84

"Do not be anxious about anything, but in everything, by prayer and petition, with thanksgiving, present your requests to God. And the peace of God, which transcends all understanding, will guard your hearts and your minds in Christ Jesus."

- anxious:

- petition:

- thanksgiving:

- hearts:

- minds:

Rewrite the verses using your findings:

In your own words, how should we come to God in every situation?

BOOK 2 - LETTING THE HEALER HEAL

Psalm 51:16-17 NIV84

"You do not delight in sacrifice, or I would bring it; you do not take pleasure in burnt offerings. The sacrifices of God are a broken spirit; a broken and contrite heart, O God, you will not despise."

- sacrifice:

- broken spirit:

- contrite:

- heart:

Rewrite the verses using your findings:

In your own words, what does God require for us to be able to come to Him for restoration?

Hebrews 4:15-16 NIV84

"For we do not have a high priest who is unable to sympathize with our weaknesses, but we have one who has been tempted in every way, just as we are—yet was without sin. Let us then approach the throne of grace with confidence, so that we may receive mercy and find grace to help us in our time of need."

- grace:

- confidence:

- mercy:

Rewrite the verses using your findings:

In your own words, how should we approach the throne of God?

Psalm 62:5-8 NIV84
"Find rest, O my soul, in God alone; my hope comes from Him. He alone is my rock and my salvation; He is my fortress, I will not be shaken. My salvation and my honor depend on God; He is my mighty rock, my refuge. Trust in Him at all times, O people; pour out your hearts to Him, for God is our refuge."

- salvation:

- honor:

- trust:

- pour:

- hearts:

Rewrite the verses using your findings:

In your own words, what should we do with the contents of our hearts?

LESSON 3   THE PURGE

Life Application

You might wonder how this skill can be applicable to you if you come from an intact home and your story is not like one in this book. The main point is that we all have hurts and pain.

> **I HAVE SAID THESE THINGS TO YOU, THAT IN ME YOU MAY HAVE PEACE. IN THE WORLD YOU WILL HAVE TRIBULATION. BUT TAKE HEART; I HAVE OVERCOME THE WORLD.**
> **—JOHN 16:33 ESV**

Suppose one of your friends unknowingly offends you. Due to a misunderstanding in communication between the two of you, instead of talking to you about it, you find out your friend has spoken to other friends about the problem. Your feelings are hurt by her words and actions. As time goes on, you realize a growing distance between you and your friend has developed, and whenever her name is mentioned in conversation, something dark and unpleasant happens in your heart. This is a good indicator you have unresolved hurt and unforgiveness that needs to be given to God before you take another step (Mark 11:25-26).

You won't be able to handle this situation in a godly way if you don't let Jesus deal with the hurt or "wound" first. By talking to God about this, He will guide you into truth amidst your hurt feelings, leading you not to sin in your anger and hurt.

God wants our vulnerability. It is key that we learn to depend on Him more than on anyone else, no matter the degree of woundedness or sin. Unchecked hurt feelings are a playground for the enemy!

WRITING YOUR HURT LETTER

You may already know what you want to pour into this letter or you may need guidance from the Holy Spirit. Either way, as you prepare for the letter, I have listed some Scriptures on the next page to focus on to help quiet yourself before the Lord.

YOU DON'T HAVE TO COME FROM AN ABUSIVE BACKGROUND TO BE WOUNDED.

1. You'll need peace and quiet.

2. Start with the WAR method of prayer, dedicating this time to Jesus Christ alone. End by asking God to place His protection around you and to lead you to the place He would like you to clean out first.

   In starting this journey of healing, it's important to learn to become fully present with God. Start with some words of worship. Worshiping your heavenly Father will always bring you into the Father's presence as well as push back the darkness, helping you hear more clearly.

   Prayer Example . . .

   Father, I praise You and thank You for Your faithfulness to me.
   Father, I ask that You intensify Your presence with me and show me
   where You want me to begin this cleansing process. I dedicate this
   time to Jesus Christ and Jesus Christ alone. Father, please place your
   hedge of protection around me and all that pertains to me.
   I only want truth as I submit myself to You for cleansing.
   Thank You for Your faithfulness to me! Amen.

   When you ask Jesus where He would like you to begin, you are allowing Him to show you where the problems are. This may come in the form of a memory, a thought that comes seemingly out of nowhere, or a picture that pops into your mind. It may be something from your childhood or something that happened this morning. Trust that the Lord is directing you to your starting point, because of the prayer above. God cares about your hurts no matter how small or silly they might seem on the outside. The key is to be transparent with Him and He will honor you for it.

3. Start writing. Just let the feelings flow out to the One who can handle it all!

   You may come back to this process many times. I have a journal full of Hurt Letters to God. Some are big and some are small; some are from my past that surface from time to time and some are from hurts that I deal with in my day-to-day life. This is a tool designed to help you learn to pour your heart out to God. You may feel spent and worn out after handing all of your baggage over to Him—that's normal. Embrace the process and rest when you feel it is needed. If you allow yourself to get overly exhausted, the effort will be lost.

   We will learn *what* to do with these letters in the lessons ahead.

4. You will need your letter to complete the next few lessons. However, if your letter hasn't come yet, keep praying and claim truth. Jesus is patient and kind. He knows your worries. Start out by writing to Him about what your worries are. He will take it from there. Remember it's not the author of this book you are trusting, it's Jesus and what you have been learning about Him through Scripture. Sometimes the hardest step is the first one, but You can trust Jesus to be there.

HELPFUL SCRIPTURE

- "Trust in Him at all times, you people; pour out your hearts to Him, for God is our refuge"(Psalm 62:8 NIV).

- "Search me, O God, and know my heart; Try me and know my anxious thoughts; And see if there be any hurtful way in me, and lead me in the everlasting way"(Psalm 139:23-24 NASB).

- "For his anger lasts only a moment, but his favor lasts a lifetime! Weeping may last through the night, but joy comes in the morning"(Psalm 30:5 NLT).

- "…nothing in all creation is hidden from God's sight. Everything is uncovered and laid bare before the eyes of Him to Whom we must give account"(Hebrews 4:13 NIV).

- "Pour out your heart like water before the presence of the Lord! Lift your hands to Him . . ."(Lamentations 2:19).

- "The Spirit of the Lord God is upon me, because the Lord has anointed me to bring good news to the poor; he has sent me to bind up the brokenhearted, to proclaim liberty to the captives, and the opening of the prison to those who are bound; to proclaim the year of the Lord's favor, and the day of vengeance of our God; to comfort all who mourn; to grant to those who mourn in Zion—to give them a beautiful headdress instead of ashes, the oil of gladness instead of mourning, the garment of praise instead of a faint spirit; that they may be called oaks of righteousness, the planting of the Lord, that he may be glorified"(Isaiah 61:1-3 ESV).

- "Enter his gates with thanksgiving, and his courts with praise! Give thanks to him; bless his name! For the LORD is good; His steadfast love endures forever, and his faithfulness to all generations"(Psalm 100:4-5 ESV).

- "To our God and Father be glory for ever and ever. Amen"(Philippians 4:20 NIV).

SPECIAL NOTE: People healing from traumatic abuse or loss should seek professional Christian counseling. Jesus IS the Healer, but sometimes we need trained individuals to walk us through hard memories and things we don't understand.

Review

1. We act in obedience when we share with God the yucky things we think we are hiding in our hearts. He wants to know us intimately. He tells us to do this throughout Scripture. As we learn to trust Him with our deep pain and disappointments, we begin to depend on Him in greater ways, turning to Him first for our security, worth, and value.

2. Be transparent. Be honest. To make our hearts good, we must clean out the junk (Matthew 12:33).

3. This letter is just between you and God. It's not intended to be given to anyone or shared with the group, unless you so choose. (Remember: Anytime you can share, it could bring healing to your heart and encourage others.)

4. The best way to move past angry and hurt feelings is to talk to God about them. Unchecked hurt feelings are a playground for the enemy!

5. Writing Hurt Letters to God is simply another form of communication or prayer to Him.

6. Remember: When you want to run away from life's problems, run to God in this very effective way!

Main Take-Away

What was your main take-away from this lesson?

Before Your Next Meeting

1. Try to have a Quiet Time at least four times this week using the verses listed for Lesson 4.

2. Memorize **Proverbs 18:21** this week.

3. Come prepared having finished Lesson 4.

CULTIVATING Holy Beauty

Women's Authentic Discipleship
It's That Simple!

Everything You Need to Get Connected!

Register with CHB to Get Updates on New Book Releases, Events, and Other News!

Help us connect women looking to join a Cultivating Holy Beauty group in your area! Scan code to register!

www.CultivatingHolyBeauty.com/Register

Training Videos for Leaders

Scan code to learn more about starting a CHB group and for answers to commonly asked questions!

https://youtube.com/channel/UCbq_TztU9UDVAazw-OLVy7g

Notes

LESSON 4

Flip It

KEY POINT
Becoming a woman of the Word helps us know God's character. The more we learn how Jesus treated those around Him, the easier it is for us to recognize His voice when He speaks to us.

WHY THIS MATTERS
The Word is only Truth—no lie can stand within it. If we know the Word, we will be armed with the Sword of Truth and be better prepared for battle! Learning to identify the difference between the Truth God speaks to us, and the lies of the enemy, is the beginning of your journey to true and lasting freedom in Jesus Christ.

HOW TO APPLY
You apply this skill by asking God to help you identify the lies in your Hurt Letter, flip the lie for Truth, then anchor that Truth with Scripture.

Leader's Guide

LESSON 4

Flip It

MEMORY VERSES
Proverbs 18:21 (Write your memory verse in the space below.)

QUIET TIME VERSES
Proverbs 18:21; Matthew 5:14-16; James 4:7-8; 2 Corinthians 10:4-6; 1 Corinthians 10:13; John 10:14-21; John 8:31-36

Complete Lesson 4 and try to have four to seven Quiet Times before your next meeting. The verses provided above are for additional Quiet Times after you have completed this lesson. To ensure you are using the verse in the correct context, be sure to read several verses before and after the suggested Quiet Time passage(s).

KEY POINT
Becoming a woman of the Word helps us know God's character. The more we learn how Jesus treated those around Him, the easier it is for us to recognize His voice when He speaks to us.

WHY THIS MATTERS
The Word is only Truth—no lie can stand within it. If we know the Word, we will be armed with the Sword of Truth and be better prepared for battle! Learning to identify the difference between the Truth God speaks to us, and the lies of the enemy, is the beginning of your journey to true and lasting freedom in Jesus Christ.

HOW TO APPLY
You apply this skill by asking God to help you identify the lies in your Hurt Letter, flip the lie for Truth, then anchor that Truth with Scripture.

Leader's Notes

- This lesson may take two weeks to complete. Remember to encourage your group members to go slow and focus on the process and not the end result. Use additional Scripture verses from the lesson for extra Quiet Time resources as needed.

- PRAY for your group to not only hear truth from the Lord but believe it in their hearts as well! This lesson is about victory in their everyday battles. Be faithful to encourage them; they will need your prayer covering!

- Stay true to teaching the Word, letting the Holy Spirit do the hard work!

- As Hurt Letters are shared in the group, listen with an ear to hear any unidentified lies. If an unidentified lie is discovered, simply ask the person something like, "Does that sound like something God would say about His precious child?"

- Anytime you can provide Scripture to anchor a truth you are speaking over someone is a win! Always try to backup any advice or encouragement you give with God's Word. It will carry more weight!

- Highlight one or two questions from the lesson to be discussed in group time, allowing each person to share an answer. For quick reference, write the page numbers of the questions you chose to discuss below.

Navigating Your Group Time

- Spend 15-20 minutes in worship.
- As the time of worship comes to a close, the leader should begin the WAR method of prayer.
- Write a quick summary of Lesson 4 in the space below.

- Ask everyone to share their "Main Take-Away" from the end of the lesson.
- Have each person share a Quiet Time.
- Ask if there are any questions about the process of identifying lies and claiming Truth.
- Have each person share from the things they learned through the exercise of flipping lies for Truth on page 79-80.
- The "Helpful Scriptures" section on page 81, is provided for added clarity and support of knowing Truth!
- If time allows, have each person share an answer from the questions the leader highlighted (1-2 questions).
- Read sections: "Review" and "Before Your Next Lesson".
- Break into pairs and recite your verses.
- Remind everyone to sign off on each other's course record in the back of the book.

Participant's Guide

LESSON 4

Flip It

MEMORY VERSES
Proverbs 18:21 (Write your memory verse in the space below.)

QUIET TIME VERSES
Proverbs 18:21; Matthew 5:14-16; James 4:7-8; 2 Corinthians 10:4-6; 1 Corinthians 10:13; John 10:14-21; John 8:31-36

Complete Lesson 4 and try to have four to seven Quiet Times before your next meeting. The verses provided above are for additional Quiet Times after you have completed this lesson. To ensure you are using the verse in the correct context, be sure to read several verses before and after the suggested Quiet Time passage(s).

KEY POINT
Becoming a woman of the Word helps us know God's character. The more we learn how Jesus treated those around Him, the easier it is for us to recognize His voice when He speaks to us.

WHY THIS MATTERS
The Word is only Truth—no lie can stand within it. If we know the Word, we will be armed with the Sword of Truth and be better prepared for battle! Learning to identify the difference between the Truth God speaks to us, and the lies of the enemy, is the beginning of your journey to true and lasting freedom in Jesus Christ.

HOW TO APPLY
You apply this skill by asking God to help you identify the lies in your Hurt Letter, flip the lie for Truth, then anchor that Truth with Scripture.

Participant's Notes

- This lesson takes courage, but it's courage that God has already provided for you! Dare to believe you are worth more than the lies you've believed! You are worth the fight!

- This week, as you work through the lesson, PRAY for yourself and your fellow group members to not only hear truth from the Lord but believe it in their hearts as well! This lesson is about victory in their everyday battles. Be faithful to encourage them; they will need your prayer covering!

- Complete this lesson before your next meeting. Be sure to answer the questions marked with a 💬 and be ready to share your answers with the group. It's important to remember there are no wrong answers to the questions throughout the lessons because they are your thoughts, so be free in how you answer!

- Use the space provided in the margins to take notes, write down additional Scripture references you find or to draw pictures that come to mind while you are learning to "Flip It." This is a powerful lesson! It's high-time to start defeating those lies you've been battling with final Truth!

- Believing the promises of God over the lies of the enemy is a choice we make daily—and a vital one at that! Stand strong in Truth, the Word of God never returns void!

Flip It

. . . AND TO PROCLAIM FREEDOM FOR THE CAPTIVES . . .
—Isaiah 61:1 NIV

Yvonne had been struggling with unkind thoughts about herself more often than usual, causing her to sink deeper into depression. Bearing the burden of caring for a child with special needs was hard enough, and lately her son seemed to be going backwards faster than he was progressing forward in his speech. At eight years old, he was growing increasingly more and more frustrated with himself and others when he couldn't communicate his needs clearly. He would often take his frustration out on Yvonne during one of his meltdowns and she would come away feeling like a complete failure. She felt inadequate to parent him. She was beginning to question her abilities as a mother and took her frustrations to God in a Hurt Letter.

> *Father,*
> *Are You sure You made the right choice when You gave my son to me? I don't know if I am doing enough for him! We are in therapy and he sees counselors, but God, he isn't improving much and he seems to be growing more and more frustrated—with everything. I feel so alone and like no one understands what I'm dealing with. I can't do this! I don't know how to help him. I'm overwhelmed with the details of this task. I'm completely ill-equipped for this! Father, my heart breaks for him! Why does he have to suffer like this? God, please help me! Help me help him, please!*

Later, after Yvonne had continued to pray throughout her day, she felt convicted over what she had written in her letter to God. She knew some of those thoughts were not true, so she went back to the letter and asked God to help her see truth. She got out a highlighter and marked anything God showed her that wasn't of Him.

Father,

Are you sure you made the right choice when you gave my son to me? I don't know if I am doing enough for him! We are in therapy and he sees counselors, but God, he isn't improving much and he seems to be growing more and more frustrated—with everything. I feel so alone and like no one understands what I'm dealing with. I can't do this! I can't help him! I'm overwhelmed with the details of this task. I'm completely ill-equipped for this! Father my heart breaks for him! Why does he have to suffer like this? God, please help me! Help me help him, please!

Yvonne then began rewriting the letter, flipping the lies for God's Truth. Honestly on her own, she was not enough for her son, but she wasn't on her own. She had the God of all creation on her side. She then began writing Scripture references in the letter after she changed the lie to Truth. This was the final step in yanking up those lies by the roots and getting herself firmly planted in truth.

Father,

Are you sure you made the right choice when you gave my son to me? I know You made the right choice when you gave my son to me, this was Your plan from the beginning! **"For I know the plans I have for you,"** declares the Lord, **"plans to prosper you and not to harm you, plans to give you hope and a future"** (Jeremiah 29:11).

I don't know if I am doing enough for him! I will seek You Father, and You will guide my steps! **"Cast your burden on the Lord, And He shall sustain you; He shall never permit the righteous to be moved"** (Psalm 55:22).

We are in therapy and he sees counselors, but God, he isn't improving much and he seems to be growing more and more frustrated —with everything. I feel so alone and like no one understands what I'm dealing with. Father, I know You are here with me, and you will never leave me! **"For I hold you by your right hand—I, the LORD your God. And I say to you, Don't be afraid. I am here to help you"** (Isaiah 41:13).

I can't do this! I can't help him! With Your help and strength I can do this. **" I can do all things through Christ who strengthens me"** (Philippians 4:13).

I'm overwhelmed with the details of this task. <u>*Although I may be overwhelmed with the details of this task, You Father, are not!*</u> **"Do not be anxious about anything, but in every situation, by prayer and petition, with thanksgiving, present your requests to God. And the peace of God, which transcends all understanding, will guard your hearts and your minds in Christ Jesus"** (Philippians 4:6-7).

I'm completely ill-equipped for this! <u>*Maybe so, but in my weakness You are strong!*</u> **". . . My grace is sufficient for you, for My power is made perfect in weakness."** Therefore, I will boast all the more gladly about my weaknesses, so that Christ's power may rest on me" (2 Corinthians 12:9).

Father my heart breaks for him! Why does he have to suffer like this? God, please help me! Help me help him, please! **"We know that God works all things together for good for the ones who love God . . ."** (Romans 8:28).

Father forgive me for listening to the enemy and choosing to entertain lies rather than truth. I know you chose me to be his mother for a reason. I know you will help me help him every day, every hour, every minute, every second, and every moment in-between! I will prove myself faithful to You. I love You!

Love,
Yvonne

Not only do these letters clean out the junk, but they help us identify how the enemy speaks to us. I mentioned in Book 1, "Intimacy with Jesus" how I believe, in general, we as believers have become more attuned to hearing and believing the enemy's lies than we have God's Truth about who we truly are. The enemy takes a truth and twists it ever so slightly in the beginning, and every time we agree with him he gives the screw another turn, causing his lie to be securely anchored into our thoughts.

Becoming a woman of the Word helps us know God's character. The more we learn how Jesus treated those around Him, the easier it is to recognize His voice when He speaks to us (see John 10:21). This is important because **"The Word of God is living and active. Sharper than any double-edged sword, it pierces even to dividing soul and spirit, joints and marrow; it is able to judge the thoughts**

and intentions of the heart" (Hebrews 4:12 NIV). The Word is only truth, no lie can stand within it. If we know the Word, we will be armed with the sword of Truth and be prepared for battle!

> **PRAISE BE TO THE LORD MY ROCK, WHO TRAINS MY HANDS FOR WAR, MY FINGERS FOR BATTLE.**
> **—PSALM 144:1 NIV**

UNDERSTANDING THE PURPOSE OF A LIE

Satan, in his least offensive form comes as a lie, like a thief in the night stealing our joy and crushing our faith. However, his ultimate goal is always to steal, kill, and destroy (see John 10:10). The main purpose a lie serves is keeping you separated from your Maker. The last thing the enemy wants you to understand is that our real value, *our true worth* hung on the cross for us.

If Satan can keep us from realizing that our true worth is the very life of Jesus, then he succeeds in keeping us from stepping into the power that was transferred to us through the Spirit of God—made available to believers when Jesus died. Jesus gave His very life so we could live! Jesus hanging on the cross is our value, and there is no way to measure the worth of that Truth! When we truly realize this we begin to win the unseen war being waged against us by flipping words like "worthless" to "priceless"!

Lies are like the soldiers that make up Satan's army. If you picture his army made up of a bunch of lies, all it takes to defeat them is to shine the light of truth on them, and poof, they are gone! All enemies of God have a weakness, and all we need to defeat this foe is to focus on the Truth of Jesus Christ—the Word made flesh! (See John 1:14).

> **WE DEMOLISH ARGUMENTS AND EVERY PRETENSION THAT SETS ITSELF UP AGAINST THE KNOWLEDGE OF GOD, AND WE TAKE CAPTIVE EVERY THOUGHT TO MAKE IT OBEDIENT TO CHRIST.**
> **—2 CORINTHIANS 10:5 NIV**

Hold onto that image of a now weakened army of Satan's lies. Have you ever wondered what it really means to "take a thought captive?" Picture one of those traitorous thoughts as a soldier from the enemy squadron on assignment. Its only task is to come in and try to set up camp starting with your mind and eventually working its way into the headquarters, turning out the lights in your heart. The enemy does this subtly with his lies by replacing your joy with depression, your love with hate, your peace with anxiety and worry, your goodness with hurt or evil, your kindness with selfishness and hostility, your faithfulness with betrayal, your patience with agitation or laziness, your gentleness with harshness, and your self-control with indulgence. In war, you always have an extreme conflict of interest as described above. If Truth is the opposite of a lie and light is the opposite of dark, then God is life and Satan is death, plain and simple. These enemy soldiers called "lies" come for one purpose and one purpose alone—to separate you from God. If we don't know the Truth written in our Bibles of how good our heavenly Father is, then we become a hostage to the evil one.

I once read a news article about how federal agents don't learn to spot counterfeit money by studying the counterfeits. They study genuine bills until they master the look of the real thing. This is our most important assignment as women of the Word! By knowing the Truth, we will be able to pull down a lie before it sets itself up as a stronghold between us and God. We don't learn how to identify darkness by studying darkness—we identify darkness by making ourselves experts of light!

Identify ways in your life where you have focused more on darkness than on the light.

IDENTIFYING AND SHUTTING DOWN ENEMY CAMPS WITHIN YOU

Ever wonder why you hide thoughts or feelings from God that you just don't want to deal with? It's an enemy soldier trying to set up camp—a lie, an evil spirit, a demon—call it whatever you like! At some point we believed the lie that God would only be pleased if we only allowed Him to see our good parts—that it's not a big deal if we keep putting off the moral issues we know we need to face.

As we experience how God treats these issues when we surrender that enemy camp to Him, He becomes a safe place for us to be our true selves, becoming more and more real to us Himself, and we learn to lean on Him first, running to Him at the first sight of an enemy soldier. The light within us starts to grow, overthrowing the darkness and begins to captivate others as we become like "a city on a hill" (see Matthew 5:14).

💬 Why does Satan want you to believe his lies? What might he gain? (John 10:10)

Learning To "Flip It"

When Yvonne shared with her Bible study group what she had learned as she prayed back over a Hurt Letter to God, one friend pumped the air with her hands and yelled, "FLIP IT!" This became one of their favorite things to say anytime they heard someone in the group speak a lie over themselves. Someone would say, "FLIP IT!" and they would all help her flip the lie for the truth. This became a powerful weapon against the enemy, where no ground could be gained!

Based on James 4:7, when we do not submit to God, Satan gains authority in our lives to harass

> **WHEN WE DO NOT SUBMIT TO GOD, SATAN GAINS AUTHORITY IN OUR LIVES TO HARASS US.**

BOOK 2 - LETTING THE HEALER HEAL

us. When we agree with the lies—Satan's native tongue (see John 8:44) —we are ultimately agreeing with him by not submitting to God. It's as if we are committing treason against God in our disobedience and giving our authority to Satan, just as Adam and Eve did. It's hard to blame them, when we continue to do the same thing they did over and over by listening to the enemy and not God.

> **JESUS SAID, "IF YOU HOLD TO MY TEACHING, YOU ARE REALLY MY DISCIPLES. THEN YOU WILL KNOW THE TRUTH, AND THE TRUTH WILL SET YOU FREE.**
> **—JOHN 8:31-32 NIV84**

THE EXERCISE

This exercise is designed to identify the lies you have allowed to overwrite God's truth in your heart. If you were able to write a Hurt Letter in the previous lesson, follow Yvonne's example of flipping lies on pages 73-75.

- Begin by praying over your letter. Ask God to point out anything not true, highlighting words that do not sound like something Jesus would say to someone He loves.

- **NOTE:** Sometimes we are so conditioned to hear bad things about ourselves it's hard to believe God wants to talk to us and tell us good things. If you are finding it hard to hear anything good, pretend this letter was written by one of your best friends. What thoughts in this letter would you never want said about her? Highlight them and tell her what God would say about those hurtful things!

- Ask God to tell you the truth about that thought and write this truth in the margin next to the lie.

- Usually there is a common theme to the lie and it can be completely destroyed with Scripture. In your Internet browser, type in for example, "verses about feeling overwhelmed." You should get a list of options. Choose one that feels most like a healing salve to your wound and write it in by the truth you replaced the lie with.

- This is the process of allowing God to rewrite lies we have believed or spoken over ourselves with truth. Practice this in your Hurt Letter now.

I had a hard time believing God would say something nice to me in the beginning. The enemy really had me trapped in a lie! But in the same way that shocking, kind words came into my mind as I searched for truth to save me from drowning, God told me to read the letter like it was about a good friend. He encouraged me to tell her what was a lie and why it was a lie. **This was a major turning point for me in my relationship with God.** This is truly when I began to fall in love with Him. He cared enough to talk with me and stretch my mind enough to find my way out of the darkness. As much as I would like to say He came and stared down my enemy, He didn't . . . what He did was even better. He trained me how to fight my battles using the weapons He provided. He taught me how to wield His sword! In my weakness, He came for me; He trained me, and in that place, He became undeniable to me.

> **BUT HE SAID TO ME, 'MY GRACE IS SUFFICIENT FOR YOU, FOR MY POWER IS MADE PERFECT IN WEAKNESS.' THEREFORE I WILL BOAST ALL THE MORE GLADLY ABOUT MY WEAKNESSES, SO THAT CHRIST'S POWER MAY REST ON ME.**
> **—2 CORINTHIANS 12:9 NIV**

💭 Looking at the findings from the exercise above, what were the common lies you heard throughout your Hurt Letter? List the most common ones here.

💭 What Scripture stood out to fight off the lie? Write it out with the reference below.

HELPFUL SCRIPTURES

- ". . . For what do righteousness and wickedness have in common? Or what fellowship can light have with darkness? What harmony is there between Christ and Belial [Satan]? What does a believer have in common with an unbeliever? What agreement is there between the temple of God and idols? For we are the temple of the living God. As God has said: 'I will live with them and walk among them, and I will be their God, and they will be my people.' 'Therefore, come out from them and be separate, says the Lord. Touch no unclean thing, and I will receive you.' 'I will be a Father to you, and you will be my sons and daughters, says the Lord Almighty" (2 Corinthians 6:14-18 NIV).

- "The people were all so amazed that they asked each other, 'What is this? A new teaching—and with authority! He even gives orders to evil spirits and they obey him'" (Mark 1:27 NIV).

- ". . . Do not give the devil a foothold" (Ephesians 4:27 NIV).

- "Never let the sun set on your anger or else you will give the devil a foothold" (Ephesians 4:26-27 JER).

- ". . . Do not give the devil an opportunity" (Ephesians 4:27 NASB).

- ". . . Do not make room for the devil" (Ephesians 4:27 NRSV).

- "Sow for yourselves righteousness, reap the fruit of unfailing love, and break up your unplowed ground; for it is time to seek the LORD, until He comes and showers righteousness on you" (Hosea 10:12 NIV84).

Review

1. Begin this exercise by asking God to help you identify lies in your Hurt Letter.

2. After you have flipped the lie, remember to utilize the Internet by typing in the search field the truth you are looking to anchor with Scripture, such as: "verse about I am a daughter of the King." This is a quick way to get many verses concerning your topic.

3. Flipping lies for God's truth is an important step in learning how God feels about us.

Main Take-Away

What was your main take-away from this lesson?

Before Your Next Meeting

1. Try to have a Quiet Time at least four times this week using the verses listed for Lesson 5.

2. Memorize **1 John 1:8-9** this week.

3. Come prepared having finished Lesson 5.

Notes

Notes

LESSON 5

Repentance and Forgiveness

KEY POINT

Learn how to move into true repentance with God, which is critical for greater intimacy with Him. As your heart becomes pure before the Lord, you will draw closer to Him.

WHY THIS MATTERS

As you grow deeper in your relationship with your Heavenly Father, you begin to trust His goodness on deeper levels. Understanding that God truly is merciful and does not desire to punish you, but desires to help you move into true and pure repentance, helps you receive His forgiveness and extend that same forgiveness to others.

HOW TO APPLY

As you work your way through this lesson, you will learn of God's immeasurable love and compassion for you as His child. You will see how He moves in your life with great acts of kindness leading you into right standing with Him.

Leader's Guide

LESSON 5

Repentance and Forgiveness

MEMORY VERSES

1 John 1:8-9 (Write your memory verse in the space below.)

QUIET TIME VERSES

1 John 1:8-9; Luke 17:1-4; Titus 3:1-11; Luke 7:44-50; Acts 3:17-19; Romans 2:1-8; Acts 17:30-31

Complete Lesson 5 and try to have four to seven Quiet Times before your next meeting. The verses provided above are for additional Quiet Times after you have completed this lesson. To ensure you are using the verse in the correct context, be sure to read several verses before and after the suggested Quiet Time passage(s).

KEY POINT

Learn how to move into true repentance with God, which is critical for greater intimacy with Him. As your heart becomes pure before the Lord, you will draw closer to Him.

WHY THIS MATTERS

As you grow deeper in your relationship with your Heavenly Father, you begin to trust His goodness on deeper levels. Understanding that God truly is merciful and does not desire to punish you, but desires to help you move into true and pure repentance, helps you receive His forgiveness and extend that same forgiveness to others.

HOW TO APPLY

As you work your way through this lesson, you will learn of God's immeasurable love and compassion for you as His child. You will see how He moves in your life with great acts of kindness leading you into right standing with Him.

Leader's Notes

- This lesson may take two weeks to complete. If a group member has to miss, causing the group to sit longer than 2 weeks in a lesson, find a time to meet with her one-on-one or over the phone so the group can keep moving forward.

- PRAY for your group to allow God to convict their hearts of any sin and unforgiveness.

- Stay true to teaching the Word, letting the Holy Spirit do the hard work!

- Highlight one or two questions from the lesson to be discussed in group time, allowing each person to share an answer. For quick reference, write the page numbers of the questions you chose to discuss below.

Navigating Your Group Time

- Spend 15-20 minutes in worship.
- As the time of worship comes to a close, the leader should begin the WAR method of prayer.
- Write a quick summary of Lesson 5 in the space below.

- Ask everyone to share their "Main Take-Away" from the end of the lesson.
- Have each person share a Quiet Time.
- Reiterate the **SPECIAL NOTE** on page 96 and 97.
- Discuss the Life Application story on page 99 and the importance of talking things through with God. If necessary consult a spiritually mature friend before addressing certain topics with others.
- If time allows, have each person share an answer from the questions the leader highlighted (1-2 questions).
- Read sections: "Review" and "Before Your Next Lesson".
- Break into pairs and recite your verses. Encourage accuracy as the Word is our greatest weapon!
- Remind everyone to sign off on each other's course record in the back of the book.

Participant's Guide

LESSON 5

Repentance and Forgiveness

MEMORY VERSES
1 John 1:8-9 (Write your memory verse in the space below.)

QUIET TIME VERSES
1 John 1:8-9; Luke 17:1-4; Titus 3:1-11; Luke 7:44-50; Acts 3:17-19; Romans 2:1-8; Acts 17:30-31

Complete Lesson 5 and try to have four to seven Quiet Times before your next meeting. The verses provided above are for additional Quiet Times after you have completed this lesson. To ensure you are using the verse in the correct context, be sure to read several verses before and after the suggested Quiet Time passage(s).

KEY POINT
Learn how to move into true repentance with God, which is critical for greater intimacy with Him. As your heart becomes pure before the Lord, you will draw closer to Him.

WHY THIS MATTERS
As you grow deeper in your relationship with your Heavenly Father, you begin to trust His goodness on deeper levels. Understanding that God truly is merciful and does not desire to punish you, but desires to help you move into true and pure repentance, helps you receive His forgiveness and extend that same forgiveness to others.

HOW TO APPLY
As you work your way through this lesson, you will learn of God's immeasurable love and compassion for you as His child. You will see how He moves in your life with great acts of kindness leading you into right standing with Him.

Participant's Notes

- Complete this lesson before your next meeting. Be sure to answer the questions marked with a 💬 and be ready to share your answers with the group.

- It's important to remember there are no wrong answers to the questions throughout the lessons because they are your thoughts, so be free in how you answer!

- As you work through the lesson this week, PRAY for yourself and your group members to allow God to convict their hearts of any sin and unforgiveness they may be harboring.

- As your faith in God's goodness grows, so will your courage to let go of the past as you choose to no longer be defined by bad choices or things that were out of your control.

- Use the space provided in the margins to take notes, write down additional Scripture references you find, or to draw pictures that come to mind as you learn how to see people the way God sees them in "Repentance and Forgiveness."

- Don't allow yourself to be isolated by the enemy. Purpose to keep in touch with your group through texts or phone calls between meetings.

- Be sure to make notes of any questions you may have for your group leader. You can also send us an email with any questions or concerns you have. We would love to hear from you and point you to Jesus any way we can! **hello@CultivatingHolyBeauty.com**

Repentance and Forgiveness

It had been seven months since Erin's husband had confessed that he had been with a prostitute, and things seemed to be getting a little better. Her husband had been addicted to pornography since he was a young teen, but now, in his early forties, he had taken it to the next level. For years, he had resisted clicking the link to meet with one of the girls on the website, but one day when he was feeling particularly stressed and all alone, he gave in. The couple had since been in counseling and things were progressing in a good direction, yet Erin still wondered if she would ever be able to fully heal and trust him again.

Recently, Erin felt God was asking her to forgive the prostitute. However, she didn't feel it was her place to forgive and she refused to think or pray about it, shutting the idea out of her mind altogether. Erin felt entitled to the pain and anger and did not want to let it go. But as the weeks progressed, Erin realized she felt distant from God; her Quiet Times didn't seem to be as satisfying, causing her mood to worsen. The days seemed to be darker and bleaker, her hope and strength were waning. ("**. . . There is no health in my body; my bones have no soundness because of my sin. My guilt has overwhelmed me, like a burden too heavy to bear . . .** " (Psalm 38:3-4 NIV).

Desperate for the gulp of air that came with deep intimacy with God, she went to Him in prayer and asked for help. (**"Ask and it will be given to you . . ."** (Matthew 7:7-8 NIV). He reminded her of the unforgiveness in her heart that was beginning to take over, causing a hardened heart toward her husband and Him. She wept as she confessed she had no idea how to forgive this woman and asked Him for help in what felt like an impossible task. Erin was tired and now truly wanted to forgive the prostitute—especially if it meant this distant feeling would leave. She knew it was necessary to heal, but had no idea where to start. (**"You're blessed when you're at the end of your rope. With less of you there is more of God and his rule"** (Matthew 5:3 MSG).

So she waited, still and quiet, for her faithful heavenly Father to lead her. (**"I believe; help my unbelief"** (Mark 9:24 ESV). She needed to see the woman as God saw her. He showed Erin that, as a child, the woman did not start out with childhood desires of being a prostitute when she grew up. He helped her see that once upon a time, Erin and the prostitute had quite a few things in common.

When they were little girls, they both wanted to be loved and cherished by a "Prince Charming" someday. They each dreamed about a "Knight in Shining Armor," a beautiful house with lots of ponies in the yard, and babies to push around in carriages. When they were little, they hoped for the same things when they grew up—being loved and cherished.

Erin felt her heart soften ever so slightly for the little girl, but she still wasn't ready to forgive. As Erin continued to think about what the Lord was showing her, she wondered what might have happened to that little girl to make her life turn out so differently from her own? What would make a woman who might have once dreamed of being a veterinarian or an astronaut believe prostitution was her only option?

Erin began to see this woman the way God saw her . . . as wounded and broken, neglected and abused. (**"When he saw the crowds, he had compassion for them, because they were harassed and helpless, like sheep without a shepherd"** (Matthew 9:36 ESV). It must have taken some kind of horrible hurt and pain to make a woman feel that the world of pornography and prostitution was her only hope. A cold chill went down Erin's spine as she wondered what kind of frightening things the enemy must have planted in the other woman. (**"We aren't fighting against human enemies but against rulers, authorities, forces of cosmic darkness, and spiritual powers of evil in the heavens"** (Ephesians 6:12 CEB).

What would this woman's Hurt Letters to God look like? Her heart began to ache for the once little girl, for her pain . . . for the now broken and wounded woman. Erin began to sob as she realized what the little girl must have gone through. Erin confessed to God for being judgmental of the truly broken girl and being unwilling to forgive. In her heart, Erin extended the forgiveness she had just received from God to the prostitute and prayed for her salvation and release from her captors.

GOD WANTS YOU TO SUCCEED!

In Erin's story, God shows us how forgiving someone by seeing them through His eyes—afflicted, harassed, helpless—like sheep without a shepherd, leads to true and lasting freedom. God allowed Erin's heart to earnestly hurt for the girl by helping her to see the truth. By God displaying His character in this compassionate manner, Erin was led to repentance, resulting in freedom and healing in her heart. Problems and past hurts don't just go away if they are forgotten about. They linger in our hearts and can seem to be gone until something bumps up against them, and the pain reminds us they are still there.

Forgiveness is always a heart issue, and mind-over-matter won't cut it! The enemy's plan is to keep us numb to the hurt and pain on the surface, while bitterness, despair, anger, self-hatred, and unforgiveness take root underneath. However, God's plan is complete restoration and healing through forgiveness—bringing true freedom!

. . . GOD'S KINDNESS LEADS YOU TOWARD REPENTANCE. —ROMANS 2:4 NIV

In Mark chapter 5, we learn of a woman who had been bleeding for twelve years. She had spent all her money on doctors, but instead of getting better, she grew worse. I can imagine feeling like being at the end of your rope—helpless, hopeless, and lost! But that wasn't the end for her! "Hope" Himself had walked into town and she believed what she heard about Him. She believed if she reached for him and touched Him, she would be healed—and she was healed!

This is another illustration of God's kindness leading us to repentance. At the end of the story, Mark 5:33 says, "Then the woman, knowing what had happened to her, came and fell at His feet and trembling with fear, **told Him the whole truth**" (emphasis added). In His kindness, Jesus healed her. He didn't have to do it that way, but it's who He is and it led her to confess the "whole truth."

God, in His infinite kindness, performs miracles like this throughout Scripture and in our own lives today. He didn't have to help Erin see the prostitute the way He saw her. He could have just demanded repentance from her and then punished her when she could not give it sincerely. But He didn't. He took her by the hand and gently led her to the truth. When she saw the truth, she believed it, repented, and was able to heal in her marriage through the sincere forgiveness she was able to extend.

Through prayer, whether in the written form of a Hurt Letter or just sitting in quiet conversation with Him, God wants to extend this same kindness to you! He desires to gently lead you into repentance so that you may be healed of *all* your afflictions. You just need to believe! The goal of this lesson is to allow God to reveal any hidden sin between you and Him, in order to be free of it. If you are struggling at this moment, God in His kindness will show it to you if you allow Him access. But you have to be willing to reach for Him in belief, as the woman in Mark chapter 5 did.

> Why do you think God chooses to act this way?

> Do you believe He will act in a similar way for you?

UNDERSTANDING THE TERMS

Repentance and forgiveness go hand-in-hand but they are not the same thing. Jesus had nothing to repent of because He was sinless. He never hurt anyone with hateful thoughts, words, or actions. However, when He hung on the cross, He became the definition of forgiveness.

> JESUS SAID, "FATHER, FORGIVE THEM, FOR THEY DO NOT KNOW WHAT THEY ARE DOING.
> —LUKE 23:34 NIV

With His body, Jesus paid the price for the sins of the entire world, past and present—even for those who hate Him. When you confess or repent of your sin by pouring out your heart to God, whether through a Hurt Letter or another form of prayer (see Psalm 62:8), you are activating the *power* of what Jesus did for you on the cross—making His pain and suffering worth the cost and not in vain.

Forgiveness is the gift you receive when you repent from a broken and contrite heart. As a daughter of the One True King, being in right standing with our Father requires repentance!

Sin causes a break in your fellowship with God. Based on 1 John 1:9, you are forgiven by the Father when you agree with Him that you are in error and take responsibility for your sin. It's at this point that your fellowship with God is restored. "But your iniquities have separated you from your God; your sins have hidden His face from you, so that He will not hear" (Isaiah 59:2 NIV).

You don't get kicked out of God's Kingdom for making mistakes, but when sin is left unchecked, it may hinder your prayers (see Isaiah 59:2, 1 Peter 3:12, and James 4:3). When you have trouble hearing Him or feel like He isn't hearing you, it's not because He is punishing you, although feeling apart from Him does feel like the worst kind of punishment for those who love Him! It's the distressing distance you feel from God that causes a hunger in those who love Him to get back to the refuge of His heart. You have the gift of forgiveness waiting for you when you take ownership of your sin! This is battle and you are a warrior in God's army! Extending forgiveness, which is the message of the cross, is the most powerful weapon you can wield against Satan.

In some cases, it will only be necessary to forgive the person in your heart. This would include forgiving someone who had passed away, as well as forgiving an abuser, or a person who is not repentant. In the latter situations, it is good to keep safe boundaries in place. Extending forgiveness does not mean the relationship will be or needs to be restored with them—it means your fellowship with God is restored.

I pray this helps you see how to pray for those who are not repentant, as they are living a life apart from God. When God tells us to bless those who curse us and pray for our enemies, what better antidote could we ask for? We are praying that our enemies would turn their hearts to God and be saved! That means they would be repentant for the wrongs they have committed and turn from their evil ways, no longer sinning against God and hurting people. Remember what we discussed in Lesson 1, that hurt people, hurt people (Matthew 12:35). It's also wise to ask God questions like Erin did: "What must have happened to make this person think this was okay or the only way?" To truly forgive we must see people the way Jesus sees them—as broken and hurting. It's heartbreaking to see people living out the evil inside their hearts, knowing the hope and love they are missing out on by living apart from God.

SPECIAL NOTE: *It's important to understand that while forgiveness is necessary in all cases, it is not the dismissal or condoning of another person's sin. God is the author of justice; trust Him to take care of the rest.*

> **IF WE CONFESS OUR SINS, HE IS FAITHFUL AND JUST TO FORGIVE US OUR SINS AND TO CLEANSE US FROM ALL UNRIGHTEOUSNESS.**
> **—1 JOHN 1:9 NIV**

In Luke 17, Jesus tells the disciples a parable comparing bitterness and unforgiveness to a mulberry (*sycamine*) tree. After doing some research, I learned this particular kind of tree has a fast-growing root structure that quickly creeps its way down, deep into the earth, making it hard to kill. Another interesting fact is, in Egypt, the harvested wood of the mulberry tree was preferred for building caskets! This tree flourishes in less than ideal situations, requiring very little water to grow. Jesus likened bitterness and unforgiveness to this very same tree—are you getting the picture now? We must not let this tree take root in us, hardening our hearts and devouring our soft inner contents like a cancer.

When discovering these insights, I'm so thankful there is always a "*But God*" moment! *But God* said all you have to do is have a little faith and tell that tree to go jump into the ocean! (See Luke 17:6).

This is where our Hurt Letters to God can be so beneficial. As we talk through these hurtful situations with God, He reveals Truth—where we went wrong or where another person may have sinned against us. Most often these root systems have crept into place without our knowing. It's not until your "Lack of Oxygen" warning light goes off that you realize you are trapped underneath the already hardened surface of your heart, created by bitterness and unforgiveness.

KNOW THE WORD! WE CAN'T PRACTICE WHAT WE DON'T KNOW, AND WE WON'T EXPERIENCE THE FRUIT OF WHAT WE DON'T PRACTICE.

By asking God to clean out our hearts in these letters, as David did in the Psalms, He directs us to the places in our hearts where these mulberry seeds were planted by the enemy—when we gave him permission by agreeing with his lies. As God shines His light in these dark places, we discover where we need to repent.

Once we receive His forgiveness, we can then extend that forgiveness where it is needed. Before we can forgive, we must receive forgiveness—we receive forgiveness through repentance.

For example, if you were a victim of child abuse, ask God to purge you of any bad thoughts (lies) about yourself that you gave into because of the abuse. Perhaps, you thought you were the cause of the abuse, or you still hold anger in your heart toward the person who abused you.

SPECIAL NOTE: *You are NOT accepting responsibility for the abuse; under no circumstances is abuse of any kind ever acceptable or justified! What you are accepting responsibility for is coming into agreement with Satan about your lack of self-worth or any other lie you may have believed in your heart as a result of the abuse. Remember, your WORTH hung on the cross for you. The very life of Jesus is your value—which is immeasurable and cannot be taken from you!*

💬 **After asking God for forgiveness, do you have a hard time believing you are actually forgiven?**

💬 **If so, try asking God to help you see yourself the way He sees you. Write out your thoughts.**

USING YOUR CONCORDANCE AND DICTIONARY, LOOK UP THE WORDS BELOW.

- unforgiveness (Matthew 6:14-15):

- bitterness (Ephesians 4:31-32):

If you were able to write a Hurt Letter in Lesson 2, read back over it and ask God to show you any issues of unforgiveness needing to be addressed. Using your journal or the space below, write out anything that sticks out or may stand between you and God, including any unresolved heart issues you find.

Extend forgiveness where it is needed. This does not always mean forgiving someone face-to-face, or even over the phone, or through a letter. Ask God how He intends for you to extend forgiveness—whether He means for you to go to someone in person or if it just needs to be done in your heart, as with Erin's story. Remember: Upon forgiveness, the door to your prison cell is opened. It's up to you to walk out of it and live from the abundance of your freedom.

Life Application

Sarah was in the process of allowing God to help her address unforgiveness in her life. She wanted to be completely rid of any sinful roots and was looking for anywhere she needed to extend and ask forgiveness. God had convicted Sarah of participating in gossip with some friends. She felt so good after repenting to God, that, in her zeal, she went to the woman she had gossiped about to ask her forgiveness. The problem was, the woman did not know she was being talked about, and it ended up deeply hurting the woman when Sarah confessed.

The better course of action might have been to go to the group she was gossiping with and ask their forgiveness for participating in the gossip and not imitating Christ. Make sure to ask God to lead you in forgiveness, whether asking for it or extending it to others. Test the answer in prayer, against the Word, and with a mature believer to make sure you are making the right choice. Be sure to follow all the way through.

> **WE CANNOT EXTEND WHAT WE HAVE NOT RECEIVED FROM GOD. BEFORE WE CAN FORGIVE, WE MUST RECEIVE FORGIVENESS—WE RECEIVE FORGIVENESS THROUGH REPENTANCE.**

After hearing Sarah's story, do you think it's wise to test your plans for reconciliation when God reveals unforgiveness in your life?

💬 Choose someone to talk through your decision before moving forward. Who will help you stay focused on Jesus' plan when it comes to safe boundaries for extending and receiving forgiveness?

💬 Does forgiving someone mean they don't have to answer for the sin they committed against you?

Review

1. It's God's kindness that leads us to true repentance (see Romans 2:4). Jesus won't ask you to do something He has not already done.

2. When extending forgiveness, it's not always necessary to do so face-to-face, unless God is pressing that on your heart.

3. What matters most is the condition of your heart. Before going to someone to ask forgiveness, make sure it is under conviction from God, and not just to unburden yourself.

Main Take-Away

What was your main take-away from this lesson?

Before Your Next Meeting

1. Try to have a Quiet Time at least four times this week using the verses listed for Lesson 6.

2. Memorize **Galatians 2:20-21** this week.

3. Come prepared having finished Lesson 6.

Notes

LESSON 6

Forgiving Self

KEY POINT
Grasp the truth that Jesus died on the Cross for you. He has forgiven you! It's time for you to surrender your disappointments of who you were not designed to be and walk into your God-given identity.

WHY THIS MATTERS
The only way to lasting freedom is through Jesus Christ.

HOW TO APPLY
Learn to see yourself the way Jesus sees you by fully accepting the forgiveness of Jesus Christ.

Leader's Guide

LESSON 6

Forgiving Self

MEMORY VERSES
Galatians 2:20-21 (Write your memory verse in the space below.)

QUIET TIME VERSES
Galatians 2:17-21; Philippians 3:12-21;1 Samuel 16:6-13; 1 Peter 5:6-7; Psalm 103:10-11; Romans 8:1-4; Psalm 103:1-14; 1 Corinthians 6:19-20

Complete Lesson 6 and try to have four to seven Quiet Times before your next meeting. The verses provided above are for additional Quiet Times after you have completed this lesson. To ensure you are using the verse in the correct context, be sure to read several verses before and after the suggested Quiet Time passage(s).

KEY POINT
Grasp the truth that Jesus died on the Cross for you. He has forgiven you! It's time for you to surrender your disappointments of who you were not designed to be and walk into your God-given identity.

WHY THIS MATTERS
The only way to lasting freedom is through Jesus Christ.

HOW TO APPLY
Learn to see yourself the way Jesus sees you by fully accepting the forgivness of Jesus Christ.

Leader's Notes

- This lesson may take two weeks to complete. Remember to encourage your group members to go slow and focus on the process and not the end result. Use additional Scripture verses from the lesson for extra Quiet Time resources as needed.

- PRAY for your group as they experience what may be the hardest part of healing—forgiving yourself. Encourage the women to go the distance and have the faith it will take to believe that when they ask forgiveness, they are truly forgiven.

- Highlight one or two questions from the lesson to be discussed in group time, allowing each person to share an answer. For quick reference, write the page numbers of the questions you chose to discuss below.

Navigating Your Group Time

- Spend 15-20 minutes in worship.

- As the time of worship comes to a close, the leader should begin the WAR method of prayer.

- Write a quick summary of Lesson 6 in the space below.

- Ask everyone to share their "Main Take-Away" from the end of the lesson.

- Have each person share a Quiet Time.

- Share part of your own journey when you accepted forgiveness from God and forgave yourself. Encourage each woman to share what God is revealing to them through this lesson of "Forgiving Self".

- Discuss the special message in the box at the top of page 116. Reiterate the point that God knew all the mistakes we would make and He chose to create us in spite of them.

- Set an example for how women in and out of your group should treat themselves as daughters of God.

- Read sections: "Review" and "Before Your Next Lesson".

- Break into pairs and recite your verses. Encourage accuracy as the Word is our greatest weapon!

- Remind everyone to sign off on each other's course records in the back of the book.

Participant's Guide

LESSON 6

Forgiving Self

MEMORY VERSES
Galatians 2:20-21 (Write your memory verse in the space below.)

QUIET TIME VERSES
Galatians 2:17-21; Philippians 3:12-21; 1 Samuel 16:6-13; 1 Peter 5:6-7; Psalm 103:10-11; Romans 8:1-4; Psalm 103:1-14; 1 Corinthians 6:19-20

Complete Lesson 6 and try to have four to seven Quiet Times before your next meeting. The verses provided above are for additional Quiet Times after you have completed this lesson. To ensure you are using the verse in the correct context, be sure to read several verses before and after the suggested Quiet Time passage(s).

KEY POINT
Grasp the truth that Jesus died on the Cross for you. He has forgiven you! It's time for you to surrender your disappointments of who you were not designed to be and walk into your God-given identity.

WHY THIS MATTERS
The only way to lasting freedom is through Jesus Christ.

HOW TO APPLY
Learn to see yourself the way Jesus sees you by fully accepting the forgivness of Jesus Christ.

Participant's Notes

- Complete this lesson before your next meeting. Be sure to answer the questions marked with a discussion bubble 💬 and be ready to share your answers with the group. It's important to remember there are no wrong answers to the questions throughout the lessons because they are your thoughts, so be free in how you answer!

- As you work through the lesson this week, PRAY for your group as they experience what may be the hardest part of healing—forgiving yourself. Encourage the women to go the distance and have the faith it will take to believe that when they ask forgiveness, they are truly forgiven.

- This lesson is to help you learn to embrace the precious child of God that you are—flaws and all. Be as forgiving to yourself as you would be your most favorite person on earth, be that a spouse, son or daughter, parent, or best friend. Become your favorite person to forgive!

- Use the space provided in the margins to take notes, write down additional Scripture references you find, or to draw pictures that come to mind as you begin learning how to "Forgive Self." This is a vital part of the journey.

- Don't hold back when it comes to forgiveness, especially for yourself! You may find that forgiving yourself is the hardest thing yet! Purpose to put the skills taught into practice.

Forgiving Self

My name is Chandra. Today, I finally have peace with the skin I came in. Today, I can say I actually want to be who I am. I have never been able to say that before. I think forgiveness is one of the most supernaturally powerful things on earth, second only to love. Because it is an act of love . . . it's what Jesus did on the cross. What He did stood for many things, but it all comes down to love and forgiveness. Jesus saved my life.

When I figured out how powerful forgiveness was, I sat and asked God to search my heart and show me who He wanted me to forgive next. I had forgiven my dad for leaving my mom when she was pregnant with me. I had forgiven the boy who stole my virginity without my permission. I had forgiven the girls who were mean to me in high school. But I was unprepared for who God wanted me to forgive next . . . myself.

During one of my Quiet Times, I asked God to help me know where and how to begin this process. As I waited for direction, I felt His love sweep over me and my heart grew warm and content. My mind began to wander, and I thought about getting to spend "everafter" with my heavenly Father. I thought about walking and talking with Him like Adam and Eve did in the garden. I reveled at the thought of finally getting to hear God speak clearly without all the human parts of me interfering.

Upon the thought of my humanness, my mind shifted as I pictured myself walking beside Jesus. I began to pick apart the woman who was walking beside Him. The warmth and contentment left me as I began to hope I would not have all those flaws when I got to heaven. I began to do what I always did when thinking about my self-image—I picked apart my shape, my hair, the way my voice sounded, and my smile. I thought about all the bad things I had done and how undeserving I was of anything good from God.

Disgust crept into my mind as I thought about all the parts of myself I would change if I could. I thought about how I hated to be intimate with my husband, not because of him, but me. Although he only gave me compliments, I thought about "my poor husband, who *had* to be intimate with me." I didn't blame him for dabbling in pornography.

I suddenly found myself formulating a plan to get *another* new gym membership and change my diet again. Seeing my Bible and journal laying in front of me, I remembered what I had been doing. I had been praying and asking God to show me who I needed to forgive next. Realization began to dawn on me. He had just shown me where to start. I didn't just believe that I was unworthy, I believed I was worthless.

I asked God to help me, as I had no idea how to begin! What was it about me that caused those kinds of thoughts? I'd asked forgiveness for every bad thing I had ever done, but I treated myself as if Jesus had said, "No" and withheld His forgiveness from me. I knew that contradicted everything Scripture said and nullified the cross. I knew it was wrong, but still I had no idea how to believe I was forgiven. I desperately wanted to believe, but I didn't know how to get that truth into my heart. I was treating myself as if I was the one exception to Scripture, that Jesus died for everyone else but me. I started with that lie and flipped it for what I knew was true, then anchored it with this verse:

> **MY OLD SELF HAS BEEN CRUCIFIED WITH CHRIST. IT IS NO LONGER I WHO LIVE, BUT CHRIST LIVES IN ME. SO I LIVE IN THIS EARTHLY BODY BY TRUSTING IN THE SON OF GOD, WHO LOVED ME AND GAVE HIMSELF FOR ME. I DO NOT TREAT THE GRACE OF GOD AS MEANINGLESS. FOR IF KEEPING THE LAW COULD MAKE US RIGHT WITH GOD, THEN THERE WAS NO NEED FOR CHRIST TO DIE.**
> **—GALATIANS 2:20-21 NLT**

I had come to believe Proverbs 30:5 with my whole heart—that "every Word of God is flawless". There are no exceptions in Scripture and Jesus never contradicts Himself! Wow, the enemy really had a field day with me on this one! He had worked hard to hide this truth from me! What must he be so afraid of? Suddenly, the answer dawned on me! The enemy was afraid of my freedom! He liked me powerless and truly believing Jesus died for everyone but me! Game over enemy soldier.

It was time to extend the forgiveness Jesus had given me to myself for the mistakes of my past and everything that I would never be, could never be, and was not designed to be. It was time to embrace my future and how I had been made. I had always seen myself in an earthly way, pointing out my flaws and trying to force myself to be something that was outside of my design. Whether condemning myself for the bad choices I had made, not being the right size, not having thick enough hair, hating my laugh, not being chosen by the "right" friends . . . you name it, I had beaten myself up about it.

As I thought about the woman who was walking and talking with God in His garden, my heart grew tender toward her. I realized I had been so hard on her, verbally, emotionally, and physically! She was a daughter God had created and then sent His son to *die* for, and I had treated her horribly! As I looked at myself, I saw a beautiful creation who just wanted to be loved and valued. She wanted to belong. I had thought and said things to her that I would never say to anyone else! I had made her skip meals to try to lose weight, I had physically pushed her too far, trying to get her to fit a shape she could never be. I had thought she should be something sexually that she wasn't. No one in her past had been more hurtful to her than me!

I had really treated this kind woman in a horrible way, no wonder she felt worthless! I never spoke life into her. I was constantly pointing out her faults, and never encouraging her in her holy beauty. If she broke a dish in the kitchen, I would call her names. If she made a mistake managing her money, I would tell her how irresponsible she was. I had no respect for her. I had allowed the worldly parts of me to persecute the precious godly part. She had been beaten, condemned, insulted, and ridiculed, all by me!

It was out of my reverence for the Lord that I became broken for that precious daughter of God. God showed me this! I hit my knees and pressed my face to the floor, asking God to forgive me. It had changed everything for me to see myself in the third person—the way my Father saw me—like a precious child I dearly loved who had been so wounded by another. My heart grew tender toward her and I just wanted to ask her forgiveness. I wanted to tell her she was beautiful just the way she was and everything would be okay! Suddenly, I knew she would have made better choices in the past if she had only known God's Word was meant to keep her safe, it was not the strict cold loveless law she once thought.

It was all love—only a loving God would care this much about her freedom! I wanted her to know it was good that she didn't fit into what culture deemed beautiful, because that kind of beauty isn't what shines from her and captivates those around her. I knew she just wanted to be loved and to give love. I knew this woman well, and I was ashamed that I had been so careless with my thoughts, words, and actions toward her. She had been through so much in her life and it was time to encourage her to finally be free and happy in who God had created her to be!

I wanted to get to know that part of myself better—not the part the world had so wrongly influenced, but the part of me that communed with God. I finally accepted myself as being a loved and cherished, imperfect daughter of God. "I am a *daughter* of God," I said to myself. Those words no longer bounced around in my head, but now settled securely in my heart. "I matter to my Father, even in the middle of my mistakes and outright rebellion. His love for me cannot be measured."

I asked God to forgive me for not believing in my heart that He had died for *me*. I got up off of the floor and went to my full-length mirror, ready to face this woman who mattered so much to God. I was shocked at the beauty I saw in the still imperfect figure. I met her kind eyes that were full of tears and forgiveness. I tried to find my voice, "What a beautiful daughter of God you are! I'm so sorry for judging you and hurting you all these years. Your holy beauty is breathtaking! I can't believe I haven't seen it before! Please forgive me…"

In my heart, I extended forgiveness to the parts of me that weren't ideal, that had made mistakes, and for the things I could not control. I just let them go. I pictured my grip loosening on all the things I was holding on to that weren't for me. I watched as the chains of self-image and ungodly expectations fell away until they were out of my sight. I just . . . let them go! In that moment it was like the parts of me that had pulled against each other for so long, yielded to one another, and for the first time I felt peace and harmony within my heart, soul, and mind.

It took some time to retrain how I spoke to myself as I moved forward. When I made a mistake I purposed to be kind to myself, asking God to forgive me. I became tender and respectful to the person I was becoming. I focused on moving forward and learning from my mistakes but not dwelling on them. For the first time in my life, I felt true peace inside. Thank you, Father, for making me!

Love,
Chandra

💬 What would it mean for you to feel this level of kindness and forgiveness toward yourself?

💬 How might learning to respect yourself as a daughter of God affect the way others see you and treat you?

> DO NOT CALL SOMETHING UNCLEAN
> IF GOD HAS MADE IT CLEAN.
> —ACTS 11:9 NLT

In 1 John 3:20, it's clear your heart (thoughts and feelings) will condemn you—but God is greater than your heart! His word is supreme. He is the final authority! When you ask God to forgive you from a pure heart, He makes you clean. You should not go on acting otherwise. What you should do is forgive yourself and move on, which is often easier said than done!

> PURIFY ME FROM MY SINS, AND I WILL BE CLEAN;
> WASH ME, AND I WILL BE WHITER THAN SNOW.
> —PSALM 51:7 NLT

I believe this is why God tells us to pour out our hearts to Him throughout Scripture. The pain of not living up to who we thought we should be, and the shame of our past mistakes all need to be cleansed by God. David refers to this process when he says "Wash me" in Psalm 51:7. A cleansing is taking place, a surrender allowing the Lord to wash impurities away as only He can do. Being close to Jesus is the only way to receive this. Be willing to allow God to take you through the process of cleansing by spending time with Him in His Word, listening as much as you talk to Him, pouring out your heart to Him in Hurt Letters, and allowing Him into your hurt places.

I believe the sinful woman of Luke 7:36-50 must have experienced something like this. Though Scripture doesn't go into detail as to *why* she was weeping at Jesus's feet to the point that she washed His feet with her tears and kisses, I would say that this was her act of surrender to Him out of deep love and reverence for *who He was*. She went into the house of Simon the Pharisee, where she knew she was not welcome and would be judged. She made herself vulnerable to Jesus and poured out everything she had. I wonder if she was convicted by the sheer closeness of proximity to Him? I know the closer I get to Jesus and the deeper my love grows for Him, the more convicted I become about the things in my life that are standing between us.

In Luke 7:50, Jesus sends her out saying, "Your faith has saved you; go in peace." Likewise, He told the woman who had been bleeding for twelve years the same in Mark 5:34, "Daughter, your faith has healed you. Go in peace and be freed from your suffering." Understand, this is all about belief without doubt in Jesus! It takes faith to truly believe with your heart that the promises of Jesus are actually meant for *you*! It takes faith to believe more is at work than just what you see with your physical eyes day-to-day. It takes faith to believe you are loved and forgiven by the One who spoke the universe into existence! Those who put their faith in Jesus and not in the things of the world will be saved, healed, and set free. This kind of faith produces a life of peace—no matter what trials come your way!

What would it mean to truly believe that Jesus actually died so you could be forgiven and live in peace?

Letting Go

Jesus came for one purpose—that we all may be saved. Spending the rest of eternity with Him in heaven is not all there is, He wants freedom for you now! He doesn't want you living under condemnation and guilt. You have the beautiful choice of letting the Healer heal you and turning away from what has held you in bondage. This can be harder than it sounds.

> **BROTHERS AND SISTERS, I DO NOT CONSIDER MYSELF YET TO HAVE TAKEN HOLD OF IT. BUT ONE THING I DO: FORGETTING WHAT IS BEHIND AND STRAINING TOWARD WHAT IS AHEAD, I PRESS ON TOWARD THE GOAL TO WIN THE PRIZE FOR WHICH GOD HAS CALLED ME HEAVENWARD IN CHRIST JESUS.**
> **—PHILIPPIANS 3:13-14 NIV**

It's a choice to let go of the past and press on toward the future with Jesus. Paul had to walk this same road as he explains in Philippians 3:13-14. God used the example of the Apostle Paul to make an impact on us—the one who condoned the torture and murder of countless Christians for the purpose of impact! If Paul could believe the love and forgiveness of Jesus was meant for him, then we all should be able to believe it for ourselves. To step into our future, we must let go of the past. It does not mean we should suppress the past and hope it goes away. Only through Jesus can you receive total freedom. To live in freedom, we must let go of guilt and shame. Let God be glorified through your past and in your everyday lives as a testimony to others!

Making the Choice

It's important to remember that no matter what your past, present and future holds, God chose you, knowing every decision you would ever make! God gave great thought and detail in creating the very same you that is here today. He knew every choice you would ever make and He still chose to create you anyway! The very hairs on your head are numbered! Even now, He thinks of you, cares for you, and longs to be closer to you. Knowing everything in your past, present and future, you are still His precious child. I understand these words may sound comforting, but they also may seem hard for you to fully believe, especially if you have experience with shame and guilt.

> Daughter,
> I knew before I created you what you would choose in that dark moment . . . and I still wanted you. I have forgiven you.
>
> Love,
> Your Heavenly Father

💬 What is the hardest part to accept about yourself, physically or otherwise?

💬 Ask God how He feels about this part of you. Write anything you hear from God.

💬 What is the hardest mistake to let go from your past?

It doesn't always occur to us that God knew about the choices we would make in the darkest time of our lives, and yet He still chose to create us anyway. He is a loving Father who brought His love down to us so that we might be saved from everlasting condemnation.

💬 Close your eyes and picture Jesus holding His hands cupped in front of Him. In His hands are all the ingredients needed to specifically make you—everything from your hair color, weight, and height, to your passions, strengths, and weaknesses. As He looks lovingly at these important pieces, He sees every choice you will ever make—good and bad. With no hesitation, He breathes His life into you, deliberately forming you. What does that imagery mean to you?

💬 Knowing God knew everything about your life before He made you, will you forgive yourself for anything you aren't and may never be? Write out any disappointment you feel.

💬 Will you purpose to allow God to help you accept yourself the way He sees you?

💬 What steps can you take to allow God to help you? Why is this important?

Review

1. When you ask forgiveness from a pure heart, it's up to you to believe Jesus died for you as well as everyone else.

2. God wants to help us process the pain of not living up to who we thought we should be and the shame of past mistakes. Be willing to let Him wash you clean of the pain. This is done by spending time with Him in His Word. Listen to Him as much as you talk to Him. Pour out your heart to God and allow Him into your hurt places for the healing process to work.

3. It's a choice to let go of the past and press on toward the future with Jesus (see Philippians 3:13-14).

4. To step into your future, you must let go of your past. Believing Jesus paid your ransom is the only way to *total* freedom.

Main Take-Away

What was your main take-away from this lesson?

Before Your Next Meeting

1. Try to have a Quiet Time at least four times this week using the verses listed for Lesson 7.

2. Memorize **Proverbs 4:20-22** this week.

3. Come prepared having finished Lesson 7.

Notes

Notes

LESSON 7

Love Letters

KEY POINT
Learn how to start hearing God's love for you over the lies of the enemy.

WHY THIS MATTERS
Walking in God's love is a vital key to walking into your God-given design.

HOW TO APPLY
Now that you are building a strong foundation of God's truth with a pure heart, you can begin to choose truth and reject lies, because you know your worth is in Jesus Christ!

Leader's Guide

LESSON 7

Love Letters

MEMORY VERSES

Proverbs 4:20-22 (Write your memory verse in the space below.)

QUIET TIME VERSES

Proverbs 4:20-23; Psalm 139; Luke 1:39-56; Mark 4:21-25; Hebrews 11:1-3; Psalm 144:1-2; Romans 7:21-23

Complete Lesson 7 and try to have four to seven Quiet Times before your next meeting. The verses provided above are for additional Quiet Times after you have completed this lesson. To ensure you are using the verse in the correct context, be sure to read several verses before and after the suggested Quiet Time passage(s).

KEY POINT

Learn how to start hearing God's love for you over the lies of the enemy.

WHY THIS MATTERS

Walking in God's love is a vital key to walking into your God-given design.

HOW TO APPLY

Now that you are building a strong foundation of God's truth with a pure heart, you can begin to choose truth and reject lies, because you know your worth is in Jesus Christ!

Leader's Notes

- It's time to let the group members know they will take turns leading the lessons in Book 3, "Walking In the New." Most likely you will have some that are fearful of leading. Be quick to encourage them and not so quick to give them an out! Often times, this fear is based on a lie. Encourage them to seek the Lord about what they have to offer others who need to know Him in this way!

- Assign the group members with the lessons they are to lead in Book 3. You may choose to be strategic in assigning specific lessons to certain group members or let the lessons fall where they may. The most important thing you can do is to pray for your group members and encourage them. Don't underestimate the Holy Spirit and His desire for everyone to be a bright light for the glory of God!

- PRAY for your group to not only hear truth from the Lord but believe it in their hearts as well! This lesson is the bridge between dispelling the enemies lies and accepting the truth of how the Father thinks of His children. Be faithful to encourage them to hear from God; they will need your prayer covering!

- Begin talking with your group about the importance of passing the gift of intimacy with Jesus on to others. Intimacy with Jesus is a gift we can't keep to ourselves! There are too many women losing the battle because they don't have the proper tools to fight the accuser and win!

- Highlight one or two questions from the lesson to be discussed in group time, allowing each person to share an answer. For quick reference, write the page numbers of the questions you chose to discuss below.

Navigating Your Group Time

- Spend 15-20 minutes in worship.

- As the time of worship comes to a close, the leader should begin the WAR method of prayer.

- Write a quick summary of Lesson 7 in the space below.

- Ask everyone to share their "Main Take-Away" from the end of the lesson.

- Have each person share a Quiet Time.

- Ask if there are any questions about hearing from the Lord in this way.

- At the end of the lesson, ask if anyone has questions about hearing from God in this way. Remember John 10:27 and Luke 1:37.

- If anyone is having trouble hearing form the Lord, encourage them to spend time asking the Lord to help them continue breaking down the wall between them and Him. Encourage more Hurt Letters and as the Leader, be covering them in prayer.

- Have each person share an answer from the "Practice" on page 132-134.

- Ask if anyone would like to share their Love Letter from God. This is not required. This will help anyone who has not yet learned how the Father speaks.

- If time allows, have each person share an answer from the questions the leader highlighted (1-2 questions).

- Read sections: "Review" and "Before Your Next Lesson".

- Break into pairs and recite your verses. Encourage accuracy as the Word is our greatest weapon!

- Remind everyone to sign off on each other's course record in the back of the book.

Participant's Guide

LESSON 7

Love Letters

MEMORY VERSES
Proverbs 4:20-22 (Write your memory verse in the space below.)

QUIET TIME VERSES
Proverbs 4:20-23; Psalm 139; Luke 1:39-56; Mark 4:21-25; Hebrews 11:1-3; Psalm 144:1-2; Romans 7:21-23

Complete Lesson 7 and try to have four to seven Quiet Times before your next meeting. The verses provided above are for additional Quiet Times after you have completed this lesson. To ensure you are using the verse in the correct context, be sure to read several verses before and after the suggested Quiet Time passage(s).

KEY POINT
Learn how to start hearing God's love for you over the lies of the enemy.

WHY THIS MATTERS
Walking in God's love is a vital key to walking into your God-given design.

HOW TO APPLY
Now that you are building a strong foundation of God's truth with a pure heart, you can begin to choose truth and reject lies, because you know your worth is in Jesus Christ!

Participant's Notes

- Complete this lesson before your next meeting. Be sure to answer the questions marked with a discussion bubble and be ready to share your answers with the group. It's important to remember there are no wrong answers to the questions throughout the lessons because they are your thoughts, so be free in how you answer!

- As you work through the lesson PRAY for yourself and your group members to not only hear truth from the Lord but believe it in their hearts as well! This lesson is the bridge between dispelling the enemies lies and accepting the truth of how the Father thinks of His children. Be faithful to encourage them to hear from God; they will need your prayer covering!

- Choosing to hear something good about yourself and reject the lies can be really hard at first! However, it is one of the most powerful things you can do for your soul!

- Listening to worship music is a good way to settle your heart and your mind as you prepare to allow God to write His love on the tablet of your heart!

- Remember to be free in the worship of your good Father! Practice worshipping at home in private.

- Be brave and very courageous! You are worth it!

- Now is a good time to order Book 3, "Walking In the New" (W.I.N.).

Love Letters

Crystal was at the end of her rope. The lies that assaulted her throughout the day were becoming more than she could bear. Most often she ended up curled in a corner on the floor sobbing while her husband, unable to help, kept their young son occupied until the onslaught had passed. She was empty on the inside; her heart felt like a wasteland of dry parched earth. She and her husband had both been to prominent seminary schools and had been active in the church for years, yet she faced this assault practically every day. She assumed she was the only one whose thoughts waged war against her to this degree.

She wondered why her pain seemed so invisible and why no one wanted to help. She freely gave to those around her, yet it seemed no one wanted to invest their time in her. She was afraid to ask for help, for fear of being seen as selfish, so the lies continued to gain strength. The longer it went on, the more Crystal became convinced the lies must be true. Crystal began to lose her identity, not just as a wife and mother, but as a person. She began to question the necessity of staying alive.

In a last ditch-effort to reconnect with God, Crystal attended a women's retreat where I happened to be working. She came hoping to hear something through the speakers that would cause her heart to start beating again. As I packed up to leave, a small group of women gathered around me. I noticed Crystal stood a little farther back than the rest. With a ball cap pulled low, she watched me with an expression that I could not quite discern.

The women asked more questions about finding their identity in Jesus and not in people. I noticed tears quietly falling down Crystal's cheeks. It became clear that, what I had thought was skepticism in Crystal was really a fearful hesitation that she had finally found what she'd been looking for. As someone with a trained ear for dying souls, I heard her say, "I want that . . . I need that." She had been trying to find her identity in her husband, friends, and even other women at church.

In Crystal's journey toward intimacy with Jesus, she needed to find her identity in Him. The lies of trying to find her identity in her marriage and other people were still intense in the beginning. But as she allowed God into her hurt places, He cleaned out the infection that had festered in her heart for so long. She had her first taste of the living water that only flows from her Heavenly Father. Crystal began to find not only her identity, but her worth in Jesus, as well. She found the strength and courage to believe that God doesn't make mistakes, not even when He created *her*. Because of what she was learning in her Quiet Times, Crystal's faith and confidence grew. Hope seemed to bubble up in her like a well-fed spring. Crystal realized she had been looking at God's Word as though it was just a story from the past. She discovered the Word is just as alive and living today as her Heavenly Father is!

After a couple months of one-on-one discipling with her and sharing Quiet Times, I challenged Crystal to ask God how He felt about her. The next time we met, she sat down at our table—barely able to contain a smile. Knowing that look myself, I asked her if she had dared to *listen* for a love letter from God. A childlike blush bloomed on her cheeks and a toothy grin broke across her face as she replied, "Yes!" While giving her a moment to gather her thoughts, she looked at me with eyes full of joyful tears and said, "I was shocked that He could love me so much!"

> **MY SHEEP LISTEN TO MY VOICE; I KNOW THEM,**
> **AND THEY FOLLOW ME.**
> **—JOHN 10:27 NIV**

Jesus talks about the importance of Him knowing us and us knowing Him. He wants to be more than a story we find hope in; He wants to be undeniable to us, a real help when we find ourselves losing our battles (see Psalm 46:1). We've been learning about letting Jesus know us by giving Him our yuckiest parts. In this lesson we will learn about knowing Him on a deeper level by allowing our hearts to believe what we hear Him say—especially about our worth.

Even though Christians should know the importance of "hearing from God," many try to ignore the practice because of the fear of being led astray. We must be intentional about learning to discern how He speaks (see 1 John 4). We learn through Scripture and by remembering that anything God communicates to us will be anchored in His Word. We cannot recognize truth if we are not rooted in Truth. This is the first and most important step in knowing *how* God speaks to us. Primarily, hearing Love Letters from God is to help you grow your communication with Him and learn how He feels about you, so that you may fully walk in confidence of Who you belong to. This is a vital part of healing our identity. Only Jesus can bind up broken hearts and set captives free. He does this by rewriting lies of the enemy with His precious truth about who we are and how special we are to Him. Remember, lies serve one purpose—to keep us separated from God. Lies always come with some level of imprisonment, but there is hope! Jesus tells us, "the truth will set you free!" (See John 8:32).

> **WE CANNOT RECOGNIZE TRUTH IF WE ARE NOT ROOTED IN TRUTH.**

If you are like Crystal and me, you may find what God has to say about you shocking! I found myself wondering why I, as a child of God, was so confident in Satan's lies about me. Yet when God spoke to me words of love and affirmation, I was convinced it must be my own pride or some lying, evil spirit! I didn't realize I was giving Satan more authority in my life than God. Today, I would rather take a chance on God rebuking me for believing Him for too much, than the certainty of Him rebuking me for believing Him for too little.

> **IT WAS GOOD FOR ME TO BE AFFLICTED,
> SO THAT I MIGHT LEARN YOUR DECREES.
> —PSALM 119:71 NIV**

💬 Why do you think it's so easy to believe bad thoughts about yourself, but so hard to believe God has good things to say to you?

💬 Why might it be important to hear these things from God? How might this benefit you?

It Takes Faith

FOR NOTHING IS IMPOSSIBLE WITH GOD.
—LUKE 1:37 NIV84

As I mentioned in a previous lesson, when I think about how much faith it took for a very young, ordinary Jewish girl named Mary to believe the words she had heard from God, it helps put into perspective hearing a Love Letter from that same God. I can't imagine the ridicule and slander she experienced as her community—ripe with Pharisees—heard the news.

Despite Mary's lowly position in society, she believed what she had heard from the Lord—that she, a common girl, was miraculously pregnant with the Savior of the world! And what was her response to such news? "'I am the Lord's servant,' Mary answered. 'May it be to me as you have said'" (Luke 1:38 NIV84). Then in Luke 1:45, Scripture says, "Blessed is she who has believed that what the Lord has *said* to her will be accomplished!" (emphasis added). This verse tells us we benefit when we believe what we hear from God, because He *is* God. And He is good!

The Bible tells us Jesus did not come to condemn us; He came to save us (see John 3:17). We know it's not in His nature to tell us we are worthless, stupid, ugly, the wrong size, the wrong color, or the wrong nationality. God will never tell us we are bad children, terrible wives, awful mothers, or any other condemning thoughts that wage war against you.

I was born with a birth defect called a cleft lip and palate, so it was easy for me to believe God must have been distracted when He created me. On my darker days, I just believed He didn't care. But as I grew and became stronger in my walk with Him, I began to see the flaws in my thinking. God was waking me up to truth and teaching me His ways and His thoughts. When the dark feeling became overwhelming, I sat in prayer and asked my Heavenly Father to show me what He was doing when He spoke me into existence. I had to know! Was I really an oversight? Had He possibly been distracted? I sat in silence wanting to please Him, daring to hear how the God of the universe felt about me. As my thoughts waged war against my mind, I remembered He had been training my fingers for battle through my Quiet Times, and I chose to believe His character and allowed His words to flow.

MY FIRST LOVE LETTER FROM GOD...

Daughter,
My precious little daughter, I am making you new. You are Mine and Mine alone. I sat among the stars the day I named you, when I called you forth from the heavens. I was marveling at My galaxies—pictures no one else gets to see. I captured the essence of the galaxy when I created you little daughter, full of beauty and wonder—My child who is so big inside for Me.

Precious are you, when you seek Me. I love it when you talk to Me. I am always here and I am always listening. Never stop seeking Me, daughter! Always draw near! Come to Me for all your needs, bring Me all your worries, tell Me everything, and I will wash your sins away.

I will take care of you. I will protect you. I will provide for you, little one. You are never too far from Me, little daughter! I love You more than you can ever imagine. You are Mine and I am yours. You are Mine and I am yours. You are Mine and I am yours.

Love,
Your Heavenly Father

Because I chose to believe my Father's words to me, Satan lost substantial authority over my life that day! It was a long time before I shared that letter from my Heavenly Father with anyone. Somewhat embarrassed, I thought people would think I was conceited. But those were not my thoughts! Being a "lover of self" as mentioned in 2 Timothy 3:2 is the opposite of God's love for us. A "lover of self" is selfish and prideful and does not put others first. It tries to fill the gaps that only God can fill. But God's love is not selfish; He is selfless. His purpose is always in the best interest of His children.

The more love letters I trusted God to speak into me, the more I began to truly perceive His love for me. This is the moment when something clicked for me and my identity switched from the things of this world, to being firmly rooted in God. My identity was no longer defined by my failures, my husband's failures, my children's failures, or what culture dictated I should be, but could never achieve. I had found my true identity in the heart of God!

Practice

The Word of God is Truth and it leads us to freedom (see John 8:32). Now that you have been having consistent Quiet Times and memorizing Scripture, you have begun to learn of God's nature on a deeper level. It's good to start practicing hearing God's voice versus the condemning, misleading lies we are so accustomed to hearing. This exercise is designed to help you begin trusting God to speak words of life to you. Begin the exercise below by putting *God* as the first person (i.e., I, Me, My, Mine, Myself), and adding *you* as the second person (i.e., you, your, yours, yourself), inserting your name where you can. This exercise will help you develop an ear for how God speaks to those willing to listen.

WRITE THESE PASSAGES OF SCRIPTURE BELOW AS A LETTER TO *YOU* FROM YOUR HEAVENLY FATHER. COMPLETE THE VERSES THAT HAVE BEEN STARTED.

Follow the example completed for you in Romans 5:8.

EXAMPLE:
Romans 5:8 NIV
"... God shows his love for us in that while we were still sinners, Christ died for us."

"... I show **My** love for **you**, (insert your name) in that while **you** were still a sinner, **I** sent **My** Son to die for **you**."

Jeremiah 31:3 NIV

"The LORD appeared to us in the past, saying: "I have loved you with an everlasting love (insert your name); I have drawn you with unfailing kindness."

Complete the verse:

"I appeared to **you** in the past, saying:

Zephaniah 3:17 NIV

"The LORD your God is with you, he is mighty to save. He will take great delight in you, He will quiet you with His love, He will rejoice over you with singing."

Complete the verse:

"I, the LORD **your** God, am with **you**, (insert your name), **I** am mighty to save.

Romans 5:5-6 NIV

". . . God's love has been poured out into our hearts, through the Holy Spirit, who has been given to us. You see, at just the right time, when we were still powerless, Christ died for the ungodly."

Complete the verse:

" . . . **My** love has been poured into **your** heart (insert your name)

Romans 8:38-39 NIV

"... **Nothing can ever separate us,** (insert your name)**, from God's love. Neither death nor life, neither angels nor demons, neither our fears for today nor our worries about tomorrow—not even the powers of hell can separate us from God's love. No power in the sky above or in the earth below—indeed, nothing in all creation will ever be able to separate us from the love of God that is revealed in Christ Jesus our Lord."** (Emphasis added)

Complete the verse:

"... Nothing can ever separate **you,** (insert your name) from **My** love."

Getting Started

- Begin with worship and commit your time to the Lord Jesus.

- As you prepare for prayer time with God, you may experience feelings of doubt or unbelief, thinking God won't speak to your heart in this way. It's also common to experience feelings of foolishness, doubt, shame, guilt, and skepticism. I encourage you to reject these lies before you get started. There is no foolishness, doubt, shame, guilt, or skepticism in God. Remember, the enemy will not tell you that you are special or cherished. Satan does not speak anything *life-giving*, he speaks only death. As a precautionary measure, here is a simple warfare prayer that will help you hear truth:

    In the Name of Jesus, I reject any lie that would lead me to doubt how God feels about me. I believe I am a cherished daughter of the One who created me. He wants to tell me and show me good and perfect things about His love for me. I dedicate this time to Jesus Christ and Jesus Christ alone. Father, I choose to hear your voice, and I do not permit any darkness to be present or influence my mind. Father, I believe, help my unbelief. Amen.

> **NO ONE WHO TRUSTS GOD LIKE THIS**
> **—HEART AND SOUL—**
> **WILL EVER REGRET IT.**
> **—ROMANS 10:11 MSG**

TIPS FOR HEARING YOUR LOVE LETTER FROM GOD

1. Be willing to hear what God has to say to you. Remember how you heard the lies? They were spoken to your mind in the form of a thought . . . Love Letters from God will most often come the same way. You are choosing what you value—God's voice, over the enemy's lies. Pray Mark 9:24, "I believe, help my unbelief!"

2. Don't be afraid to let your hand write what your spiritual ears hear.

3. You may feel like you are being silly, but don't! Trust the **life** that is being spoken into you, like you once trusted the lies!

4. Write as fast as you can until the words runs out.

5. Remember that Jesus did not come to condemn you (see John 3:17). Allow God to speak His love into you.

6. This letter is just between you and God, so let the words flow through your hand and believe the Father loves you! This is a vital step to your freedom.

7. It's not necessary to share Love Letters. However, by sharing, you may help lay a foundation for others who may not have been able to hear.

8. Your first letter may be one word or ten pages. The length does not matter and doesn't reflect whether God loves you more or less than someone else. As your faith grows, so will the letters!

TIME TO TRUST AND WRITE

With pen in hand or fingers ready to type, you can start with questions like:

"Father, how do You feel about me?"

"Father, will You ever leave me?"

"Father, what were You doing when You created me?"

Most often, you will not hear an audible voice; it will seem like impressions or thoughts. One woman I discipled was so shocked the first time God spoke about His love for her, that she tore the journal entry out and threw it away! Concerned, I asked her what the letter said. She replied, "It was too kind! If anyone ever found and read it, they would think I thought too highly of myself in God's eyes!"

Again, this is another example of believing lies from the enemy about a lack of self-worth. When God speaks His truth into us, we often deny it. It's important to note there is nothing prideful or conceited in receiving a love letter from God. It's doubtful you will be tempted to embellish what you hear because it will be so humbling and perfect, but you may be tempted to hold back. Don't thwart the Spirit, just write what you hear.

My First Love Letter from God

My First Love Letter from God

Review

1. Being willing to hear love letters from God increases your confidence in how the Creator of all things feels about you. You become a spiritual force to be reckoned with, squashing the enemy's lies.

2. When transcribing Love Letters from God, don't feel foolish about what you hear.

3. Don't hold back; keep writing until the words run out.

4. There is nothing prideful in love letters from God; it's what you do with them that can lead to pride. This is truly for your confidence in Christ alone. Spur one another on and always encourage one another in the love and character of Jesus.

5. If you do not want to share your letter with the group, be sure to share it with at least one group member or someone whom you trust for godly confirmation and accountability.

6. If anyone in the group has the gift of "Word of Knowledge" (see 1 Corinthians 12:8), and you have someone struggling to hear from God, please understand this exercise is about each person hearing from God *themselves*. While giving a "Word of Knowledge" is for the edification of others, please understand the *importance* of each of us learning to hear directly from our Heavenly Father!

7. Hearing truth in this way takes faith, and you will NEVER regret it! (See Romans 10:11)

Main Take-Away

What was your main take-away from this lesson?

Before Your Next Meeting

1. Try to have a Quiet Time at least four times this week using the verses listed for Lesson 8.

2. Memorize **1 Corinthians 10:13** this week.

3. Now is a good time to order Book 3, "Walking In the New."

Notes

LESSON 8

The Power of Choice

KEY POINT
You choose what you value!

WHY THIS MATTERS
Understand you always have a choice with God. Freedom is never an option with the enemy.

HOW TO APPLY
Learn how to make the heart-illustration applicable in real time, avoiding bitterness setting in and hardening your heart.

Leader's Guide

LESSON 8

The Power of Choice

MEMORY VERSES

1 Corinthians 10:13 (Write your memory verse in the space below.)

QUIET TIME VERSES

1 Corinthians 10:6-13; 2 Corinthians 2:5-17; John 8:3-12, Proverbs 4:23-27; Deuteronomy 30:11-20; James 4:7-17; Hosea 10:12-13

Complete Lesson 8 and try to have four to seven Quiet Times before your next meeting. The verses provided above are for additional Quiet Times after you have completed this lesson. To ensure you are using the verse in the correct context, be sure to read several verses before and after the suggested Quiet Time passage(s).

KEY POINT

You choose what you value!

WHY THIS MATTERS

Understand you always have a choice with God. Freedom is never an option with the enemy.

HOW TO APPLY

Learn how to make the heart-illustration applicable in real time, avoiding bitterness setting in and hardening your heart.

Leader's Notes

- After your time of worship and prayer, take a moment to familiarize the leader's-in-training with the Leader's Guide.

- If you have not already, assign the group members with the lessons they are to lead in Book 3. You may choose to be strategic in assigning specific lessons to certain group members or let the lessons fall where they may. The most important thing you can do is to pray for your group members and encourage them. Don't underestimate the Holy Spirit and His desire for everyone to be a bright light for the glory of God!

- PRAY for your group to begin allowing God to rewrite their value system. Be faithful to encourage them; they will need your prayer covering!

- Highlight one or two questions from the lesson to be discussed in group time, allowing each person to share an answer. For quick reference, write the page numbers of the questions you chose to discuss below.

Navigating Your Group Time

- Spend 15-20 minutes in worship.
- As the time of worship comes to a close, the leader should begin the WAR method of prayer.
- Write a quick summary of Lesson 8 in the space below.

- Ask everyone to share their "Main Take-Away" from the end of the lesson.
- Have each person share a Quiet Time.
- If time allows, have each person share an answer from the questions the leader highlighted (1-2 questions).
- Discuss the heart illustration on page 149.
- Discuss the Moment of Choice, Heart Illustration on page 151.
- Read sections: "Review" and "Before Your Next Lesson".
- Break into pairs and recite your verses. Encourage accuracy as the Word is our greatest weapon!
- Remind everyone to sign off on each other's course record in the back of the book.

Participant's Guide

LESSON 8

The Power of Choice

MEMORY VERSES
1 Corinthians 10:13 (Write your memory verse in the space below.)

QUIET TIME VERSES
1 Corinthians 10:6-13; 2 Corinthians 2: 5-17; John 8:3-12; Proverbs 4:23-27; Deuteronomy 30:11-20; James 4:7-17; Hosea 10:12-13

Complete Lesson 8 and try to have four to seven Quiet Times before your next meeting. The verses provided above are for additional Quiet Times after you have completed this lesson. To ensure you are using the verse in the correct context, be sure to read several verses before and after the suggested Quiet Time passage(s).

KEY POINT
You choose what you value!

WHY THIS MATTERS
Understand you always have a choice with God. Freedom is never an option with the enemy.

HOW TO APPLY
Learn how to make the heart-illustration applicable in real time, avoiding bitterness setting in and hardening your heart.

Participant's Notes

- As you learn to walk in this new freedom from pain and unforgiveness you will grow in spirit— causing you to desire more and more, the things your Heavenly Father desires, and less the things of this world.

- Use the space provided in the margins to take notes, write down additional Scripture references you find, or to draw pictures that come to mind as you learn how to "Meditate on the Beauty of Truth."

- Begin praying for yourself and for your group members to allow God to rewrite their value system. Be faithful to stay in the Word!

- Complete this lesson before your next meeting. Be sure to answer the questions marked with a discussion bubble and be ready to share your answers. It's important to remember there are no wrong answers to the questions throughout the lessons because they are your thoughts.

- You get to choose what you value, sisters! Though you may not be able to control what comes your way, you sure can *choose* how to respond to it!

- Be brave and very courageous! You are worth it!

- Be sure to order Book 3, "Walking In the New" (W.I.N.).

- Be sure to get the name of the lessons you will be leading in Book 3 from your leader. Write them here:

- Once you receive Book 3, "Walking In the New," begin by reading the section called, "You Were Made for This!" in the front of the book to tips and guidelines.

The Power of Choice

Donnie and Selena had been married for nearly twenty years. A lot had changed over this time and they seemed to finally be getting the hang of being married. In the early years of their marriage, Donnie had often used hard and fast words or fear tactics to get control in their house, whether it be with Selena or their children. More recently, Selena had truly begun to enjoy Donnie's company as he had been pursuing God on a deeper level.

Donnie was a faithful husband, father, and hard worker. He volunteered in their church as often as possible. Although he was making great strides, whenever he became stressed he would sometimes revert to his default mode of hateful and degrading words.

One night, Selena found herself at her wits end with one of their teenagers' disrespect and bad attitude. Frustrated, Selena had turned to Donnie for help. Fed up with the state of his family, Donnie turned on Selena, all gentleness and kindness gone, and snarled, "Why don't you show your daughter how to behave by closing your own mouth, *WOMAN!* Selena knew he didn't mean it, but still she felt her heart splinter down the middle, as old scars tried to rip open. Shame and guilt for being an imperfect female tried to break through her safe boundary of Truth and set up camp. Her husband's words dripped with disgrace. Without caring that her husband and children were present, Selena squeezed her eyes shut and began to pray out loud, "Father I choose truth! I choose truth! I reject the lie that I am a failure as a woman, and that my voice doesn't matter. I reject the lie that I am Your afterthought, Your second best. My husband is not my salvation, You are my salvation, Lord. Your Blood saved me—Yours and Yours alone. Father help me cling to Your truth!

So many lies are trying to break in right now! Father, there are so many things that I don't understand in Your Word—things that I may never have answers to this side of heaven. But what I do know is that I am Yours and You are mine! Before I am anything else, whether good or bad, I am your child! Father, help me keep the walls down between me and You. Help me not to run and hide like I did before. I know You won't hurt me, Father. I know You love me. I choose Truth! Do you hear that Satan? I choose JESUS!"

In that moment, Selena had mastered the *power of choice* by choosing Jesus instead of letting the lies waylay her. Selena had been through the process of cleaning out past infection in her heart and had learned the skills of *flipping lies* and *anchoring truth* with Scripture. She was well aware of what an enemy soldier sounded like. In this area—once a battleground she lost over and over—now she was the *victor* in the Name of Jesus!

The next time Selena and I met, she brought her Hurt Letter, eager to share. She had applied all the skills of taking her pain to God, that she learned over the course of our time together. She showed me this diagram she had drawn.

"I recognized what was happening immediately," she said! "No way was I going to let that lie take root after all the work I'd done plowing it up. My heart was still hurting after I prayed and all I could think about was telling God about it. So I took my Bible and journal and started writing to God about my hurt feelings. Then I drew the heart illustration like you showed me, labeling each section from the hurtful event. From my letter, I uncovered the wound and identified the lie Satan was trying to plant.

When the moment of choice came it was really hard because I knew if I held on to the hurt I would have some semblance of control over the situation and my husband, making him suffer for the hateful things he said! I knew that wasn't godly, so I fought for the truth and then anchored it with His Word!

Selena was so excited at this point she was nearly bouncing in her chair! "It worked!" she exclaimed. "There was no bitterness, guilt, or shame! I just felt peace and delight from my Heavenly Father!" Thank you for giving me this tool allowing God to help me fight and win the battles in my marriage that I had been losing for so long!"

TAKE A MOMENT TO STUDY THE *MY BATTLE FIELD* ILLUSTRATION ON THE NEXT PAGE.

> When you find yourself struggling in the battle, sometimes taking a step back and getting Godly perspective can help. Ask the Holy Spirit to help you fill out the "My Battle Field" worksheet on page 186. This worksheet is also available in the Letting the Healer Heal Quiet Time Journal.

My Battle Field

"The heart is deceitful above all things and beyond cure. Who can understand it?"
Jeremiah 17:9 (NIV)

1. The Wound:
My husband spoke degrading words to me about my worth and value. It was also done in front of our children.

2. The Lie:
I'm a failure. My husband is a bad man who will never change! And that I should hold on to the pain of those words and punish him!

3. Moment of Choice!
Nope! God does NOT talk to me that way! **And I will not take revenge into my own hands!** (Romans 12:19) I am God's daughter—He is my strength when I am weak! (Philippians 4:13) My husband is not the enemy, Satan is. Father, please convict my husband's heart of his sin. (Ephesians 6:12)

4. The Result of My Choice:
Freedom from the enemy and when my husband asked for **forgiveness**, it came quickly into my heart.

ILLUSTRATION 2.3
Disclaimer: This illustration is an interpretative graphic of how the spiritual heart functions for the purposes of spiritual healing in Letting the Healer Heal by Jessie North. In no way should it be used in physical interpretations or to replace professional medical care. It's intended use is for the Cultivating Holy Beauty series only.

LESSON 8   THE POWER OF CHOICE   149

The Moment of Choice

STUDY THE MODIFIED HEART ILLUSTRATION ON THE NEXT PAGE FROM LESSON 1.

This illustration represents what happens when you choose the lies that weasel their way in over a wound instead of Truth. Remember: You are now cultivating a life of holy beauty by learning God's character through His written Word. Having His Word in you enables you to make the right choice!

The squiggly line of the heart illustration represents the moment in which you decide to hold your ground and choose Truth or give up that ground to Satan by believing the lie.

Sometimes you move forward by simply standing still—by holding your ground and not falling backwards. By maintaining your position after you have been hurt and not giving up any ground to the enemy—as you trust God to be your refuge—you are able to hold on to your authority in Christ. Claim His truth in your heart and be better equipped for the next battle. By choosing truth, you keep the outer rim of your heart broken and contrite, ready to receive the Good Seed of the Word in the fresh, moist soil of your heart.

The Moment of Choice

SELF-HATRED
SHAME • GUILT
WORTHLESSNESS • JEALOUSY • RAGE
ANGER • PRIDE • RESENTMENT • REVENGE
CONTROL • VIOLENCE • SICKNESS
FEAR • ADDICTION • FRUSTRATION
THOUGHTS OF SUICIDE • WORRY
ADULTERY • INSECURITY
SELF-RIGHTEOUSNESS
ANXIETY
BITTERNESS

THE MOMENT OF CHOICE

God will always give you a choice in what you believe and the direction you take. Truth or lie, love or hate, guilt or innocence, shame or honor, life or death, light or dark, God or not.

> "But when you are tempted, He will also provide a way out so that you can endure it." (1 COR 10:13).

3 This large layer represents what happens if we choose to believe the lie. When we adopt Satan's thought patterns about ourselves in place of God's truth, we enter into a cycle of sinful nature. The pus and infection caused by the lies we believed affects how we view ourselves, how we view God, how we love our husbands, raise our children, and interact with the world. We pour into others from this layer of our heart. (see *Matthew 12:34-35*)

2 Satan exploits the wound with his lies about God and our identity. This is the moment where we choose to claim truth or believe the lies from the enemy, thus determining the contents of our hearts. (see *John 10:10*)

1 The smallest area represents the real issue/s or original entry point of the wound. This could have taken place in childhood or adulthood and may include hurtful words or actions, or any type of abuse. (see *John 16:33*)

ILLUSTRATION 2.4

Disclaimer: This illustration is an interpretative graphic of how the spiritual heart functions for the purposes of spiritual healing in *Letting the Healer Heal* by Jessie North. In no way should it be used in physical interpretations or to replace professional medical care. It's intended use is for the *Cultivating Holy Beauty* series only.

LESSON 8 THE POWER OF CHOICE 151

THIS ILLUSTRATION REPRESENTS WHAT HAPPENS TO YOUR HEART
WHEN YOU CHOOSE TRUTH OVER LIES.

The Healthy Heart

LOVE JOY
PEACE · PATIENCE · KINDNESS
GOODNESS · FAITHFULNESS
GENTLENESS
SELF-CONTROL

> "Plant the good seeds of righteousness, and you will harvest a crop of love. Plow up the hard ground of your hearts, for now is the time to seek the LORD, that he may come and shower righteousness upon you" (Hosea 10:12 NLT).

ILLUSTRATION 2.2
Disclaimer: This illustration is an interpretative graphic of how the spiritual heart functions for the purposes of spiritual healing in *Letting the Healer Heal* by Jessie North. In no way should it be used in physical interpretations or to replace professional medical care. It's intended use is for the *Cultivating Holy Beauty* series only.

What you choose when Satan tries to exploit your wounds, determines what fills the portion of your heart you live from. If you choose God's Truth, then you will live from a soft and supple heart full of the fruit of the Spirit. You will pour Light into those around you, as you are able to hold on to God's plan for your life (see Jeremiah 29:11). The wound is then healed and erased, and you live in the Lord's delight as His daughter—a godly wife, godly mother, friend, and disciple-maker.

However, if you choose to believe the lie, it's like putting germs in an open wound and watching infection set in. As your heart begins to be filled with pus and scabs from the unchecked hurt and lies, the outer layer of your heart begins to harden with calluses and scabs. This makes it harder and harder for Truth to enter in as you begin to only see the enemy's plan for your life and marriage, which is destruction, divorce, and death.

> Do you see the value in stopping to take care of an emotional wound when it happens, the way you would stop and take care of a physical wound? How might this change the way you care for yourself in the future?

The Result of Choice

So far you have learned to expect pain in this life here on earth. And rightly so (see John 16:33). But it's what you do with the pain that determines the path you walk and the quality of life you live while here on earth. You have learned how to pour your heart out to God through honesty and humility, how to identify lies and "Flip It" for God's Truth, and how to anchor what you've heard from the Lord in His Word. You've also learned the vital necessity and power of repentance and forgiveness.

WE GET TO CHOOSE WHAT WE VALUE!

This lesson, "The Power of Choice," helps you understand that God always gives you a choice in how you live and what you choose to value. God will always provide a way out—it's a promise: "But when you are tempted He will also provide a way out so that you can endure it" (1 Corinthians 10:13).

Cultivating Holy Beauty and learning to walk in this new freedom from pain and unforgiveness will cause you to grow in your spirit. You will begin to desire more and more, the things your Heavenly Father desires, and less the things of this world. You get to choose what you value, sisters! Though you may not be able to control what comes your way, you sure can choose how to respond to it!

> **EVEN IF WE FEEL GUILTY, GOD IS GREATER THAN OUR FEELINGS, AND HE KNOWS EVERYTHING.**
> **—1 JOHN 3:20 NLT**

Taking thoughts captive is a powerful choice you can make, and in many cases will be life-changing! What is the most common thought or lie often plaguing you about yourself or others? Refer to your Hurt Letter if needed.

💬 Considering what you have learned about God and the way He feels about you, how do you think He feels about that lie or opinion of yourself?

💬 Writing it out below, flip the lie above for Truth and anchor it with Scripture. Write as many verses as you like to securely anchor that Truth in your heart.

💬 By turning from these lies, Satan has to flee from you (see James 4:7). Use this process every time you find a lying enemy soldier setting up camp. Ask God to place alarm bells around the old way of thinking, so that you can be reminded to choose life. Write any needed notes here.

💬 Will you CHOOSE to turn from lies by choosing Truth? Write your answer below, including the date and your signature.

LESSON 8   THE POWER OF CHOICE

Review

1. God *always* gives us a *choice* in what we value.

2. The next time your heart is hurting, take it to God as soon as you can sit down with Him. Let Him help you sort out Truth from lies using "The Hurting Heart" illustration.

3. It's just as important to take care of an emotional or spiritual wound, as it is a physical wound.

Main Take-Away

What was your main take-away from this lesson?

Before Your Next Meeting

1. Try to have a Quiet Time at least four times this week using the verses listed for Lesson 9.

2. Memorize **1 Peter 3:15-17** this week.

3. Come prepared having finished Lesson 9.

4. Now is a good time to order Book 3, "Walking In the New".

Notes

Notes

LESSON 9

Your Living Testimony

KEY POINT
Movements of God fly on the wings of testimonies—and your testimony is the life you live as a child of God in front of a lost and hurting world.

WHY THIS MATTERS
The story of your redemption through Jesus Christ is just a story if you don't live in a way that proves your faith. Living out your testimony in front of others will open doors for you to share your journey with God and bring hope to the lost and hurting.

HOW TO APPLY
The more vulnerable you are with others—the more readily they will see Jesus in you. The fruit of your faith will speak for itself.

Leader's Guide

LESSON 9

Your Living Testimony

MEMORY VERSES

1 Peter 3:15-17 (Write your memory verse in the space below.)

QUIET TIME VERSES

1 Peter 3:15-17; Philippians 1:27-30; Revelation 12:10-11; Isaiah 55:10-13; Psalm 107:1-9; Ephesians 4:1-4; Galatians 6:1-6

Complete Lesson 9 and try to have four to seven Quiet Times before your next meeting. The verses provided above are for additional Quiet Times after you have completed this lesson. To ensure you are using the verse in the correct context, be sure to read several verses before and after the suggested Quiet Time passage(s).

KEY POINT

Movements of God fly on the wings of testimonies—and your testimony is the life you live as a child of God in front of a lost and hurting world.

WHY THIS MATTERS

The story of your redemption through Jesus Christ is just a story if you don't live in a way that proves your faith. Living out your testimony in front of others will open doors for you to share your journey with God and bring hope to the lost and hurting.

HOW TO APPLY

The more vulnerable you are with others—the more readily they will see Jesus in you. The fruit of your faith will speak for itself.

Leader's Notes

- By now you should have assigned the group members with the lessons they are to lead in Book 3, "Walking In the New".

- Remind the group member assigned to Lesson 1 of Book 3, to be prepared to lead at the next meeting.

- Be sure to reach out to each participant to pray with them, encourage them, and answer any questions or squelch lies they may be hearing before it's their turn to lead.

- Ask God to help you be bold with your testimony! Be faithful to encourage them; they will need your prayer covering!

- Highlight one or two questions from the lesson to be discussed in group time, allowing each person to share an answer. For quick reference, write the page numbers of the questions you chose to discuss below.

Navigating Your Group Time

- Spend 15-20 minutes in worship.

- As the time of worship comes to a close, the leader should begin the WAR method of prayer.

- Write a quick summary of Lesson 9 in the space below.

- Ask everyone to share their "Main Take-Away" from the end of the lesson.

- Have each person share a Quiet Time.

- If time allows, have each person share an answer from the questions the leader highlighted (1-2 questions).

- Read sections: "Review" and "Before Your Next Meeting".

- Break into pairs and recite your verses. Encourage accuracy as the Word is our greatest weapon!

- Remind everyone to sign off on each other's course record in the back of the book.

Participant's Guide

LESSON 9

Your Living Testimony

MEMORY VERSES
1 Peter 3:15-17 (Write your memory verse in the space below.)

QUIET TIME VERSES
1 Peter 3:15-17; Philippians 1:27-30; Revelation 12:10-11; Isaiah 55:10-13; Psalm 107:1-9; Ephesians 4:1-4; Galatians 6:1-6

Complete Lesson 9 and try to have four to seven Quiet Times before your next meeting. The verses provided above are for additional Quiet Times after you have completed this lesson. To ensure you are using the verse in the correct context, be sure to read several verses before and after the suggested Quiet Time passage(s).

KEY POINT
Movements of God fly on the wings of testimonies—and your testimony is the life you live as a child of God in front of a lost and hurting world.

WHY THIS MATTERS
The story of your redemption through Jesus Christ is just a story if you don't live in a way that proves your faith. Living out your testimony in front of others will open doors for you to share your journey with God and bring hope to the lost and hurting.

HOW TO APPLY
The more vulnerable you are with others—the more readily they will see Jesus in you. The fruit of your faith will speak for itself.

Participant's Notes

- Use the space provided in the margins to take notes, write down additional Scripture references you find, or to draw pictures that come to mind as you learn to become bold in "Your Living Testimony."

- PRAY for yourself and your fellow group members to be bold in sharing what God has done in your life! It's through the blood of the Lamb and your testimony that the accuser is overcome (see Revelation 12:11)! Don't withhold this blessing from the hurting and lost around you. Your story could be just what they needed to hear!

- Complete this lesson before your next meeting. Be sure to answer the questions marked with a discussion bubble and be ready to share your answers with the group. It's important to remember there are no wrong answers to the questions throughout the lessons because they are your thoughts, so be free in how you answer!

- The time of worship during group time is provided for you to come fully present before the Lord, especially if you have had a busy day. There is not a wrong way to worship Jesus—whether you sit quietly, lay on the floor, dance, kneel, or raise your arms. Be free in your response to the Father!

- Make sure you have ordered Book 3, "Walking In the New."

Your Living Testimony

Evelyn had lived most of her adult life under the weight of guilt and shame from choices she had made in the past. She had been raised in a strong religious family, where rules reigned over love. The intense desire to feel loved and important to someone when she was a teenager, left her in the waiting room of an abortion clinic. Evelyn didn't think she could withstand the disappointment from her family if they found out she was pregnant. Throughout her formative years, no one ever explained to her why sex before marriage was wrong or how it could hurt her and others. Her parents and other adults had threatened that getting pregnant before marriage would "ruin your life" but they never explained why or how.

Although she now knew it was a lie from the enemy, when she found herself pregnant at eighteen, she believed abortion was her only option for freedom. She feared she would never accomplish any of her dreams if she went through with the pregnancy. Feeling as though she had nowhere else to turn, she asked a friend to drop her off at the clinic a month before she was to leave for college.

Evelyn had no idea of the prison cell waiting for her on the other side of the abortion. No one told her the baby would be the first victim, and she would be the second. No one told her it's a life she was ending for her own selfish desires and comfort. Evelyn entered into a deep, dark reality of self-hatred and depression which led to a year-long struggle of alcohol abuse as she tried to dull the pain. Feeling isolated from God and halfway across the country from her family, she dropped out of college, having lost sight of the dreams that were once so clear to her.

After a few years of working odd jobs to make ends meet, her life began to look up when she got married. When the newlywed couple discovered they were expecting, Evelyn begged God out of fear to forgive her, afraid He would punish her for the abortion by causing her to lose her baby during pregnancy. Once the baby arrived safe and sound, she then worried God would cause her to lose her child, so every night as she rocked her baby to sleep, she desperately cried out to God for forgiveness and to not take her child.

No matter how things looked on the outside, Evelyn still lived imprisoned on the inside by fear, guilt, and shame. Even though Evelyn had asked God to forgive her, she was asking out of fear and guilt. She had hoped it would just go away with time, but it hadn't. Evelyn had never believed God had forgiven her. She only cried out because she believed He would take-away her child. Anxiety and worry continued to wrack her body, causing doctors to prescribe medication to manage the symptoms.

For over a decade, Evelyn had tried to hide this past stain from herself and God, seeking to find some semblance of freedom. When she learned how to have a Quiet Time, she began to learn of God's nature. As she grew in heart knowledge of her Savior, she started to believe Scripture as it took deeper root in her. The longer she walked with God, the more the abortion from her past started to surface from the place she had stuffed it so deep inside. She had no choice but to bring it before God and deal with it once and for all—this time not out of fear, but from a repentant and truly broken heart.

Evelyn poured out her heart to God, telling Him the story and accepting responsibility for her actions. She told Him she never thought she would have considered abortion as an option, until she found herself desperate for a way out of a bad situation. She repented as tears splashed onto her journal—as her pen fell to the floor and sobs broke free from her chest. Evelyn surrendered the parts she hated about herself, fully giving her life over to the Lord. Her heart was broken for what she had done—utterly and completely shattered.

As she searched for God intently with all her senses, waiting to hear a verdict from Heaven, she saw an image play across her mind. The same fear she felt that day stole her breath as she was back on the abortion table vividly remembering a baby being torn from her womb. Just then, she saw Jesus appear beside her. He wasn't filled with hatred or rage toward her as she expected; instead, He showed great sorrow. He was weeping for her. Big, pain-filled tears ran into His beard as He bent over her explaining His love and that He had a better way for her. Evelyn sat in the moment for a while soaking in the Truth of where Jesus was. He had come to her in the abortion clinic of all places! He loved her then, in the middle of her darkest hour, and she had to *choose* to believe He loved her now. In the moment, Evelyn chose life, by choosing truth!

In His kindness of showing her this image, He had led her to repentance. Deciding it was truly the only way, Evelyn chose to believe she was forgiven by God, once and for all—truly forgiven. She sat in silence letting that reality settle in.

Sucking in a deep breath, she knew there was one last thing to do. As she sniffled away the last of her tears, she felt the deep peace of God's forgiveness wash over her! Evelyn knew she had to forgive what God had forgiven. Picturing herself sliding the chains off her arms, legs, and throat, she watched them fall into the dark pit they had been relentlessly dragging her toward. When Evelyn raised her head, she immediately noticed the weight of darkness was gone. She began living each new day with a new spirit that broadcast for all to see, I AM FORGIVEN and FREE!

Though she feared judgment and condemnation over the past, Evelyn soon began to feel the need to share her story of how God bound up her broken heart and set her free from the captor who had isolated her for so long. Evelyn's story of choosing to believe God's forgiveness was so inspiring to others, she began to get invited to speak to groups of women, young and old. She shared her testimony and explained how God became undeniable when He met her in the broken places of her life and how she had to make the hardest choice of all: The choice to receive His forgiveness *and* forgive herself.

Evelyn's journey with God was full of His great acts of mercy, forgiveness, and redemption. One night after Evelyn spoke, an older woman came up and asked if they could step outside for a moment. Fear of judgment and condemnation reared its ugly head as Evelyn was certain she had offended the woman with the details of her story. Battling fear, she brought to mind the image of Jesus holding her hand while He wept as she laid on the abortion table. The lies disintegrated as she now clung to Him, choosing truth and not doubting she was forgiven.

Evelyn sat down on the concrete steps and met the firm gaze of the woman. "I want to know how you are so confident you are forgiven," she said firmly. "I see it in your eyes, I hear it when you speak . . . you have no doubts that your abortion is as far from God as the east is from the west! You really believe that your sins have been washed away?!" With her eyes cast down, the woman said, "I need to know how to let my past go and believe that I can live in freedom from my bondage like you!"

Over the next several months Evelyn began discipling the older woman, teaching her how to make time with Jesus a priority. And soon, through learning the skill of writing Hurt Letters to God, she experienced true freedom from the lies, as God's truth became undeniable for her too.

> HERE'S WHAT I DO KNOW: I WAS BLIND AND NOW I SEE.
> —JOHN 9:25 NIV

What Is a Testimony?

The word "testimony" means "evidence given" or "proof." The story of your redemption through Jesus Christ is just a story if you don't live in a way that proves your faith. Your testimony does not end when you receive salvation. On the contrary, it just begins!

While Evelyn has a powerful story with a lot of intense elements, it wasn't her story that caught the older woman's attention. It was the way Evelyn chose to live in hope and freedom that made the woman take notice and desire what Evelyn knew in her heart.

MOVEMENTS OF GOD FLY ON THE WINGS OF TESTIMONIES.

It truly does not matter how amazing your story is if you don't live a repentant and forgiven life, bearing the fruit of the Spirit. Evelyn feared she would face persecution and judgment from others for being so transparent about the choices she made in the past, but the truth is, it was through the ugly parts of her story that God received the most glory! When Evelyn spoke of these things freely in front of the other women with confidence in what her heavenly Father had done for her, there was no denying that she had truly received the gift of God's forgiveness. The more transparent Evelyn was with her story, the more other women were able to relate to her.

> IT IS MY PLEASURE TO TELL YOU ABOUT THE MIRACULOUS SIGNS AND WONDERS THAT THE MOST HIGH GOD HAS PERFORMED FOR ME.
> —DANIEL 4:2 NIV84

As with Paul in the Book of Acts, your testimony doesn't just tell of where you have been. It was clear to everyone the type of wretch Paul was before his conversion. But it wasn't just the miraculous story of how Jesus spoke to him on the road to Damascus that made everyone take notice of Paul's new identity. It was the abrupt change in his behavior and the choices he made—his obvious heart change toward Christians.

In John 10:37-38, Jesus said, "Do not believe Me unless I do the works of my Father. But if I do them, even though you do not believe Me, believe the works, that you may know and understand that the Father is in Me, and I in the Father." This illustrates clearly that it is not just your "story" that makes up your testimony. How you live day-to-day in the present—your thoughts, words, and actions—all testify that God is in you, that He is good! Jesus is your salvation, and what better proves you genuinely believe, than how you live your life from then on!

The evidence of holy fruit in your life completes your testimony as God gives you the privilege to live and show it daily. Paul reiterates this in Ephesians 4:1 when he says, "I urge you to live a life worthy of the calling you have received." It's your life of holy beauty that speaks of God's goodness and captivates those around you, giving you opportunity to share your story!

> **BUT IN YOUR HEARTS REVERE CHRIST AS LORD. ALWAYS BE PREPARED TO GIVE AN ANSWER TO EVERYONE WHO ASKS YOU TO GIVE THE REASON FOR THE HOPE THAT YOU HAVE.**
> **—1 PETER 3:15 NIV**

One of my favorite testimonials in Scripture is that of the Samaritan woman at the well (John 4:1-42). The woman came to draw her water in the heat of the day when everyone else had gone. It appeared she would rather go in the hottest, sweatiest part of the day than have to be in the presence of the townspeople. However, when Jesus came along, there was no hierarchy between the Samaritan woman and Himself. The woman was shocked that a Jewish man would even ask her for a drink of water, which speaks of her own view of her worth.

When Jesus told her everything she had ever done, the woman was convicted and believed in who He was. This was when He began to restore her identity. He tore away even the label that demeaned her race when He explained that her worship was enough for Him! The kind of worship the Father was seeking could not be found on a mountain top or in a hierarchy of race or religion. The Father desired a heart bowed low in reverential prayer—it was a matter of the heart—a balance of spirit and truth (John 4:23-24)!

The woman took off into town to tell the townspeople about the man who had convicted her. Jesus had restored her value and worth. We know this first because she felt confident enough to go and share her testimony with the townspeople, and second because they listened!

The whole town listened to her testimony and revival broke out in Samaria! In one conversation, Jesus stripped this woman of anything that devalued her and gave back what the enemy had stolen—her identity. And as if that wasn't enough, revival broke out, and many people were saved!

> **THEY OVERCAME HIM BY THE BLOOD OF THE LAMB AND THE WORD OF THEIR TESTIMONY.**
> **—REVELATION 12:11 KJV**

💬 Is your life proving your faith in Jesus?

💬 What might the consequences be if you share your testimony without living in the commandments of God?

💬 Consider your testimony. What parts of your story will be the hardest to share?

Spiritual Assessment for Book 2

Take a moment to think back over all that has happened since you began this study, *Cultivating Holy Beauty,* and then answer the questions below.

💬 Has anything happened specifically on your journey through *Cultivating Holy Beauty* that has truly strengthened your walk with Jesus and brought about change in your life?

💬 Would you say you have a deeper relationship with Jesus now than you did before starting this journey?

💬 Do you genuinely like who you are? Explain your answer.

💬 How would you describe your spiritual life right now? Would you consider it stagnant, average, learning and growing daily or another response?

💬 How has your view of God changed since beginning *Cultivating Holy Beauty*?

💬 How do you handle battles now compared to before *Cultivating Holy Beauty*?

💬 Think back to where you were emotionally, mentally and spiritually before starting *Cultivating Holy Beauty*, what differences do you see?

Your Journey with Jesus

By comparing the questions above with the ones you answered at the beginning of this journey in Book 1, "Intimacy with Jesus" you now have a "testimony" or "evidence given" for the impact *Cultivating Holy Beauty* has had on your spiritual life! See how simple it is? Take some time to think about your journey to faith. Keeping the above questions in mind, write out a few key points from your life you would share with someone who was hurting and in need of hope.

Remember the more transparent you are with your failures and pain, the easier it will be for the people you are sharing with to relate to you. Jesus is a master at loving imperfect people. As Christians, the more we can be vulnerable with our struggles, yet walk in the fruit of the Spirit, the more we will captivate those around us for the kingdom. These key points will be what you build your story around.

Your testimony may come out a little different each time you share it. It has been my experience that depending on who I am talking with, the Holy Spirit will specifically highlight certain parts the person needs to hear.

> **DO NOT BE AFRAID; KEEP ON SPEAKING, DO NOT BE SILENT. FOR I AM WITH YOU, AND NO ONE IS GOING TO ATTACK OR HARM YOU, BECAUSE I HAVE MANY PEOPLE IN THIS CITY.**
> **—ACTS 18:9-10 NIV84**

Besides the fact that the Bible tells us to be ready to give an explanation for the hope we have, why would you want someone to hear your story? What might someone gain?

What would you recommend as the next step for someone after they prayed to receive salvation?

The Gift of a Life Transformed

I had been a Christian for nearly fifteen years before I began pursuing an actual relationship with God. As I learned to trust God's Word and His Spirit more and more, I began to experience the deep healing and freedom that only Jesus can bring.

It all started, when women from my home church—so captivated by the love and hope of Jesus radiating from my transformed heart, began asking me for help. I started discipling them one-by-one, teaching them the things I had learned and pointing them to Jesus in every situation that arose in their broken lives. I was careful to not judge them, but love them right in the middle of their mess. I shared my own failures and how Jesus—the Word made flesh—came in and made me victorious over the lies I heard and sin I chose.

The Holy Spirit began to impress upon me the need to write down the things I was learning, and even though I felt inadequate for the job, I obeyed, because I trusted Him. As time went on, I saw God glorified in the lives of the women around me as they chose to obey the commands of Jesus in Scripture.

This is the fundamental goal of *Cultivating Holy Beauty*, to glorify the Lord—exalt Him highly—by teaching His people how to love Him with all they have!

Will you join me in this? Is God using *Cultivating Holy Beauty* to teach you how to love Him more? Would you like to see other women get this same opportunity? Will you co-labor with God as He gently wakes the women around you, bringing healing and restoration to the Bride of Christ through this ministry? Will you answer the call of the Great Commission by stepping up as a disciple, who is willing to go, and make disciples?

Start praying now, and ask God to show you the women He has for you to begin leading through the *Cultivating Holy Beauty* discipleship curriculum. Ask your group leader how to get started and visit **www.CultivatingHolyBeauty.com** for more information. You were made for this! Thank you!

In His Grip,

Jessie
Author
Cultivating Holy Beauty

Review

1. Living out your testimony in front of others will open doors for you to share your journey with God and bring hope to the lost and hurting.

2. The more transparent you are about your struggles, the greater impact you will have on those listening.

3. Your testimony may come out a little different each time you share it. Trust the Holy Spirit to reveal the parts of your story the person you are speaking with needs to hear.

Main Take-Away

What was your main take-away from this lesson?

Before Your Next Meeting

1. Come prepared having finished Lesson 1 of Book 3, "Walking in the New". Try to have a Quiet Time at least four times this week using the verses listed for Lesson 1 of "Walking In the New."

2. Memorize **2 Corinthians 5:17** this week.

3. Be sure the leader assigned the group members with the lessons they are to lead in Book 3, "Walking In the New."

4. Before each group member leads their assigned lessons, you must read, "You Were Made for This! Participant Leader Notes" on page viii-ix of Book 3, "Walking in the New" followed by "Are You the Group Leader?", "Guidelines for a Successful Group," "Addressing Hard Topics," and "I Want Jesus!"

5. Read "It's Time to Lead!" on 176.

It's Time to Lead
PREPARING PARTICIPANTS FOR LEADING

> WHO KNOWS, PERHAPS YOU HAVE COME TO YOUR
> ROYAL POSITION FOR SUCH A TIME AS THIS.
> —ESTHER 4:14 CSV

Dear Group Participant,

Like Esther, you were made for such a time as this! There are women all around us, face down on the battlefield, with the lies of the enemy stabbed in their backs. It's time to rise up and shine—stepping into your rightful place on the battlefield as a leader and teaching those around you the skills to help them fight and win the battles they face every day!

In Book 3, "Walking In the New" (W.I.N.), the group participants will begin taking turns leading the weekly meetings—simply follow the Leader's Guide! You may not have realized it, but God has already been using you to minister to your fellow group members through the sharing of your Quiet Times and being transparent about your journey—failures and all.

Your group is a safe place to learn and grow not only in your relationship with Jesus, but also as a disciple-maker. If you are willing to yield to God and follow His lead, He will use you in mighty ways! All He needs is a willing vessel!

Begin asking God to prepare your heart to lead a group of your own. Don't fear! Your job is to love them well and point them to Word, letting the Holy Spirit do the rest!

Your group leader will assign the lessons you are to lead, walking with you every step of the way! Be sure to read the resources listed below found in the front of Book 3. These resources are designed to help prepare you for leading.

- You Were Made for This! Participant Leader Notes
- Are You the Group Leader
- Group Basics
- Guidelines for A Successful Group
- Addressing Hard Topics

Be bold! Be courageous! Your sisters in Christ need the skills you have learned! Remember we are fighting from victory, not for victory. Welcome to the battlefield!

Fighting from victory,

Jessie

Author
Cultivating Holy Beauty

Notes

CULTIVATING Holy Beauty
Women's Authentic Discipleship
It's That Simple!

Please Share Your Journey With Us!

I believe movements of God fly on the wings of testimonies! We would love to hear how Cultivating Holy Beauty has helped grow your walk with God!

www.CultivatingHolyBeauty.com/yourjourney

Appendix

Book 2: Letting the Healer Heal
COURSE RECORD

LESSON TITLE   **MEMORY VERSES**   **LEADER INITIAL - DATE**

Lesson 1: Healing with Jesus

Lesson 2: Faith in the Healer

Lesson 3: The Purge

Lesson 4: Flip It

Lesson 5: Repentance and Forgiveness

Lesson 6: Forgiving Self

Lesson 7: Love Letters

Lesson 8: The Power of Choice

Lesson 9: Your Living Testimony

FINAL RECORDS FOR BOOK 2

Finish All Nine Lessons

Memorize Nine Scripture Passages

Total Number of Quiet Times I've Completed

About the Author

Like many of Jesus' first disciples, I did not come into ministry with theological training or the eloquence of someone who had been taught in church from an early age. A series of hard life choices and the consequences that followed left gaping wounds in my life, exposing a heart that was spiritually dying and in desperate need of a Savior. And this is where Jesus closed the divide, drawing me to Himself through a series of dreams and revealing His plan of salvation to me. I found myself humbled, bent low at the foot of the cross. I stand victorious today only because of Jesus.

In 2013, my husband, Adam, began the ***Every Man a Warrior*** discipleship program by Lonnie Berger. It was through Christ's transformative overflow in my husband's life that God awakened me. He called me to begin writing ***Cultivating Holy Beauty*** upon realizing that lies had held me captive for over a decade *after* my salvation. As I grew in my heart knowledge of the Word, I became convinced of Proverbs 30:5, "Every word of God is flawless." Then one day, it clicked: "All of God's promises are true, and they are for me!" In that moment, my heart became like a bright city on a hillside. It was as if a light had been turned on inside me, and others wanted to know what had changed! I was being presented with one opportunity after another to share the Gospel—drawing back a shade to awaken the Bride of Christ to a Son that's already risen!

As one of His commissioned disciples, I am deeply committed to preparing the Bride for His return. I don't have an impressive résumé. I'm not rehearsed in the art of storytelling or teaching Bible studies. My only qualifier is Jesus. I am His humble servant and instrument. These words are an overflow of His work in *my* life. You can't fall in love with the Creator of the universe and keep silent! His love changes everything. I want you to *know* Him. Will you arise and join me in pursuing Him? He wants to be found (Jeremiah 29:13).

Jessie North
Daughter of the Living God, Wife, and Mother
AUTHOR
Cultivating Holy Beauty

The Quiet Time Worksheet

DATE: / /

SCRIPTURE I READ:

KEY POINT:

FAVORITE VERSE:

REWRITE THE VERSE:
In your own words and without changing the meaning

APPLICATION & PRAYER
HOW might this verse change the way you live? WHY does practicing this truth in your daily walk with God matter? Write a PRAYER to the Lord sharing what you learned and what the verse means to you.

EMPHASIZE:
Focus on different words to better understand their context and meaning.

ASK QUESTIONS:

IS THERE...

A PROMISE TO CLAIM?

A SIN TO AVOID?

A COMMAND TO OBEY?

SOMETHING NEW YOU LEARNED ABOUT GOD?

Cultivating Holy Beauty | www.CultivatingHolyBeauty.com

The Quiet Time Worksheet

DATE: /   /
SCRIPTURE I READ:

KEY POINT:

FAVORITE VERSE:

REWRITE THE VERSE:
In your own words and without changing the meaning

APPLICATION & PRAYER
HOW might this verse change the way you live? WHY does practicing this truth in your daily walk with God matter? Write a PRAYER to the Lord sharing what you learned and what the verse means to you.

EMPHASIZE:
Focus on different words to better understand their context and meaning.

ASK QUESTIONS:

IS THERE...

A PROMISE TO CLAIM?

A SIN TO AVOID?

A COMMAND TO OBEY?

SOMETHING NEW YOU LEARNED ABOUT GOD?

Cultivating Holy Beauty | www.CultivatingHolyBeauty.com

The Quiet Time Worksheet

DATE: / /

SCRIPTURE I READ:

KEY POINT:

FAVORITE VERSE:

REWRITE THE VERSE:
In your own words and without changing the meaning

APPLICATION & PRAYER
HOW might this verse change the way you live? WHY does practicing this truth in your daily walk with God matter? Write a PRAYER to the Lord sharing what you learned and what the verse means to you.

EMPHASIZE:
Focus on different words to better understand their context and meaning.

ASK QUESTIONS:

IS THERE...

A PROMISE TO CLAIM?

A SIN TO AVOID?

A COMMAND TO OBEY?

SOMETHING NEW YOU LEARNED ABOUT GOD?

Cultivating Holy Beauty | www.CultivatingHolyBeauty.com

The Quiet Time Worksheet

DATE: /   /
SCRIPTURE I READ:

KEY POINT:

FAVORITE VERSE:

REWRITE THE VERSE:
In your own words and without changing the meaning

APPLICATION & PRAYER
HOW might this verse change the way you live? WHY does practicing this truth in your daily walk with God matter? Write a PRAYER to the Lord sharing what you learned and what the verse means to you.

EMPHASIZE:
Focus on different words to better understand their context and meaning.

ASK QUESTIONS:

IS THERE...

A PROMISE TO CLAIM?

A SIN TO AVOID?

A COMMAND TO OBEY?

SOMETHING NEW YOU LEARNED ABOUT GOD?

The Quiet Time Worksheet

DATE: / /
SCRIPTURE I READ:

KEY POINT:

FAVORITE VERSE:

REWRITE THE VERSE:
In your own words and without changing the meaning

APPLICATION & PRAYER
HOW might this verse change the way you live? WHY does practicing this truth in your daily walk with God matter? Write a PRAYER to the Lord sharing what you learned and what the verse means to you.

EMPHASIZE:
Focus on different words to better understand their context and meaning.

ASK QUESTIONS:

IS THERE...

A PROMISE TO CLAIM?

A SIN TO AVOID?

A COMMAND TO OBEY?

SOMETHING NEW YOU LEARNED ABOUT GOD?

Cultivating Holy Beauty | www.CultivatingHolyBeauty.com

The Quiet Time Worksheet

DATE: /   /
SCRIPTURE I READ:

KEY POINT:

FAVORITE VERSE:

REWRITE THE VERSE:
In your own words and without changing the meaning

APPLICATION & PRAYER
HOW might this verse change the way you live? WHY does practicing this truth in your daily walk with God matter? Write a PRAYER to the Lord sharing what you learned and what the verse means to you.

EMPHASIZE:
Focus on different words to better understand their context and meaning.

ASK QUESTIONS:

IS THERE...

A PROMISE TO CLAIM?

A SIN TO AVOID?

A COMMAND TO OBEY?

SOMETHING NEW YOU LEARNED ABOUT GOD?

My Battle Field

"The heart is deceitful above all things and beyond cure. Who can understand it?" Jeremiah 17:9 (NIV)

4. The Result of My Choice:

3. Moment of Choice!

2. The Lie:

1. The Wound:

ILLUSTRATION 2.5
Disclaimer: This illustration is an interpretative graphic of how the spiritual heart functions for the purposes of spiritual healing in *Letting the Healer Heal* by Jessie North. In no way should it be used in physical interpretations or to replace professional medical care. It's intended use is for the *Cultivating Holy Beauty* series only.

My Battle Field

"The heart is deceitful above all things and beyond cure. Who can understand it?" Jeremiah 17:9 (NIV)

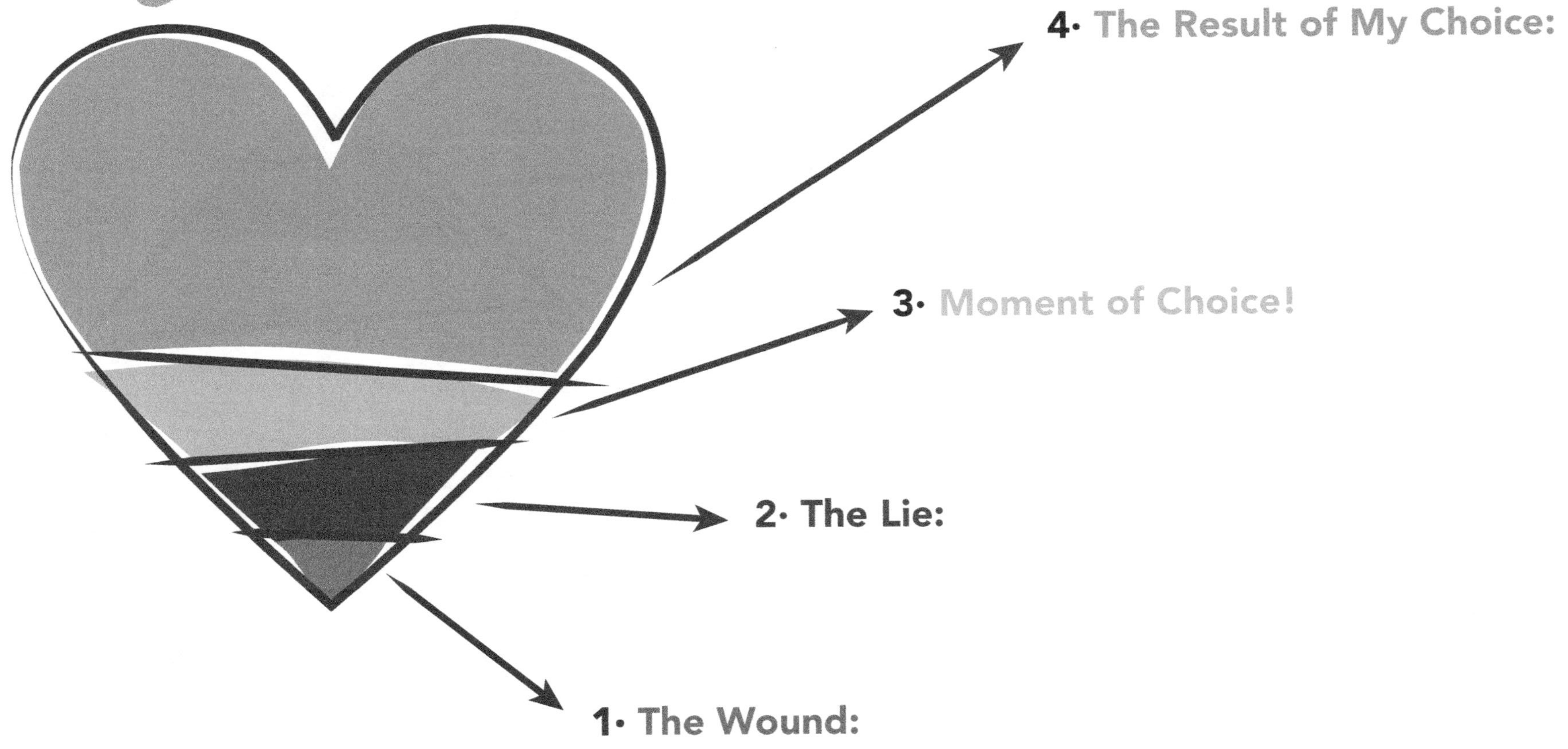

4. The Result of My Choice:

3. Moment of Choice!

2. The Lie:

1. The Wound:

ILLUSTRATION 2.5
Disclaimer: This illustration is an interpretative graphic of how the spiritual heart functions for the purposes of spiritual healing in *Letting the Healer Heal* by Jessie North. In no way should it be used in physical interpretations or to replace professional medical care. It's intended use is for the *Cultivating Holy Beauty* series only.

My Battle Field

> "The heart is deceitful above all things and beyond cure. Who can understand it?" Jeremiah 17:9 (NIV)

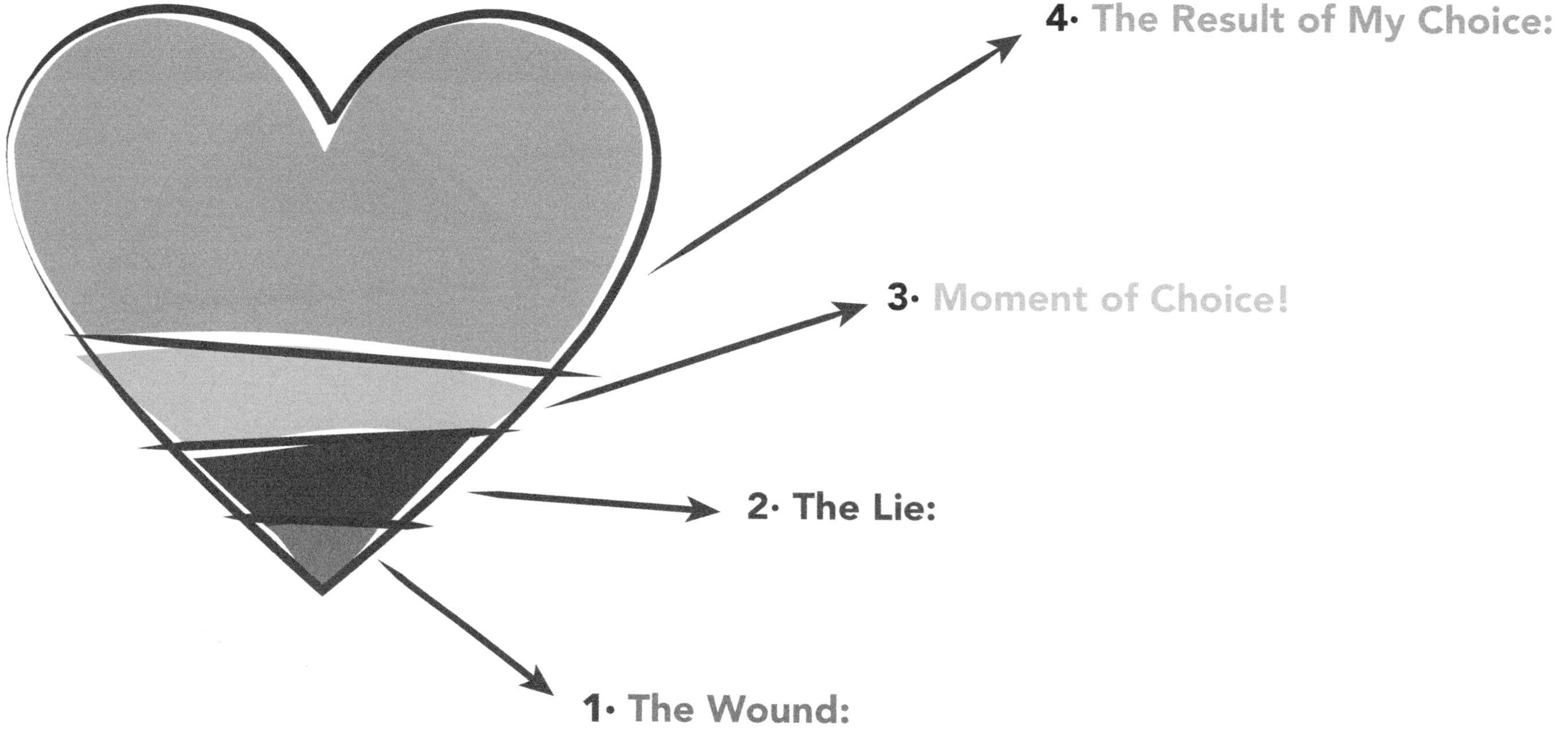

4. The Result of My Choice:

3. Moment of Choice!

2. The Lie:

1. The Wound:

ILLUSTRATION 2.5

Disclaimer: This illustration is an interpretative graphic of how the spiritual heart functions for the purposes of spiritual healing in *Letting the Healer Heal* by Jessie North. In no way should it be used in physical interpretations or to replace professional medical care. It's intended use is for the *Cultivating Holy Beauty* series only.

Cultivating Holy Beauty | www.CultivatingHolyBeauty.com

My Battle Field

> "The heart is deceitful above all things and beyond cure. Who can understand it?" Jeremiah 17:9 (NIV)

4. The Result of My Choice:

3. Moment of Choice!

2. The Lie:

1. The Wound:

ILLUSTRATION 2.5

Disclaimer: This illustration is an interpretative graphic of how the spiritual heart functions for the purposes of spiritual healing in *Letting the Healer Heal* by Jessie North. In no way should it be used in physical interpretations or to replace professional medical care. It's intended use is for the *Cultivating Holy Beauty* series only.

BOOK 2: LETTING THE HEALER HEAL

CHAPTER 1: WHY HEALING WITH JESUS IS SO IMPORTANT

Proverbs 4:23

Cultivating Holy Beauty

BOOK 2: LETTING THE HEALER HEAL

CHAPTER 2: FAITH IN THE HEALER

Luke 1:45

Cultivating Holy Beauty

BOOK 2: LETTING THE HEALER HEAL

CHAPTER 3: THE PURGE

James 1:2-4

Cultivating Holy Beauty

BOOK 2: LETTING THE HEALER HEAL

CHAPTER 4: FLIP IT

Proverbs 18:21

Cultivating Holy Beauty

CHAPTER 1: WHY HEALING WITH JESUS IS SO IMPORTANT

CHAPTER 2: FAITH IN THE HEALER

BOOK 1: LETTING THE HEALER HEAL
Scripture Memory

BOOK 1: LETTING THE HEALER HEAL
Scripture Memory

CHAPTER 3: THE PURGE

CHAPTER 4: FLIP IT

BOOK 1: LETTING THE HEALER HEAL
Scripture Memory

BOOK 1: LETTING THE HEALER HEAL
Scripture Memory

Card 1
BOOK 2: LETTING THE HEALER HEAL
CHAPTER 5: REPENTANCE AND FORGIVENESS

1 John 1:8-9

Cultivating Holy Beauty

Card 2
BOOK 2: LETTING THE HEALER HEAL
CHAPTER 6: FORGIVING SELF

Galatians 2:20-21

Cultivating Holy Beauty

Card 3
BOOK 2: LETTING THE HEALER HEAL
CHAPTER 7: LOVE LETTERS

Proverbs 4:20-22

Cultivating Holy Beauty

Card 4
CHAPTER 8: THE POWER OF CHOICE

1 Corinthians: 10-13

Cultivating Holy Beauty

CHAPTER 5: REPENTANCE AND FORGIVENESS

CHAPTER 6: FORGIVING SELF

BOOK 1: LETTING THE HEALER HEAL
Scripture Memory

BOOK 1: LETTING THE HEALER HEAL
Scripture Memory

CHAPTER 7: LOVE LETTERS

CHAPTER 8: THE POWER OF CHOICE

BOOK 1: LETTING THE HEALER HEAL
Scripture Memory

BOOK 1: LETTING THE HEALER HEAL
Scripture Memory

BOOK 2: LETTING THE HEALER HEAL

CHAPTER 9: YOUR LIVING TESTIMONY

1 Peter 3:15-17

CULTIVATING Holy Beauty

CULTIVATING Holy Beauty

CULTIVATING Holy Beauty

CULTIVATING Holy Beauty

CHAPTER 9: YOUR LIVING TESTIMONY

BOOK 1: LETTING THE HEALER HEAL
Scripture Memory

BOOK 1: LETTING THE HEALER HEAL
Scripture Memory

BOOK 1: LETTING THE HEALER HEAL
Scripture Memory

BOOK 1: LETTING THE HEALER HEAL
Scripture Memory

CULTIVATING Holy Beauty

CULTIVATING Holy Beauty

CULTIVATING Holy Beauty

CULTIVATING Holy Beauty

BOOK 1: LETTING THE HEALER HEAL
Scripture Memory

BOOK 1: LETTING THE HEALER HEAL
Scripture Memory

BOOK 1: LETTING THE HEALER HEAL
Scripture Memory

BOOK 1: LETTING THE HEALER HEAL
Scripture Memory

Made in the USA
Middletown, DE
20 October 2023